THE FUTURE
— OF —
FREELANCE

HOW TO FIND YOUR
OWN TEMPORARY JOBS

GREAT FULL-TIME WORK
EXCELLENT WAY TO FIND A PERMANENT JOB

PATRICIA BARNES

All Rights reserved.
Copyright © 2021 by Patricia Barnes

No part of this book may be reproduced or transmitted in any form or by any means, electronic or mechanical, or otherwise, including photocopying, recording, or by any information storage and retrieval system, without permission in writing from the author. Permission is given to any professional reviewer to use parts.

ISBN 13: 978-1-951772-83-3
E-book ISBN 13: 978-1-951772-95-6
Library of Congress No. TX0000891849

Limits of Liability and Disclaimer of Warranty
While the publisher and author have used their best efforts in preparing this book, they make no representation or warranties with respect to the accuracy and completeness of the contents of this book and specifically disclaim any implied warranties of merchantability or fitness for a particular purpose. No warranty may be created or extended by sales representatives or written sales material. The advice and strategies contained herein may not be suitable for your purpose. The publisher and author are not engaged in rendering professional services, and you should consult with a professional where appropriate, including but not limited to, legal and accounting services. Neither the publisher nor author shall be liable for any loss of profit or other commercial damages, including but not limited to special, incidental, consequential, or other damages.

Each web address or link contained in this book was active at the time of publication. However, because of the ever-evolving nature of the internet, links may have changed.

Publishing Coordinator – Sharon Kizziah-Holmes
Cover Design – Jaycee DeLorenzo
Headshot Photographer – Susan Scott Smith

PO Box 570821
Houston TX 77257-0821

DEDICATION

I dedicate this book to Steve Ouellette, my friend who connected me to my first Freelance Temporary assignment and who made the suggestion of doing it permanently as my full-time job.

CONTENTS

Dedication i
Acknowledgments ii
Introduction iii
1 – Temporary Work 1
2 – Your Company Name.. 7
3 – Preparing To Launch Your Business 15
4 – Should You Have A Website and Facebook Page? 25
5 – Updating Your Software Skills 27
6 – Start Your Client List 31
7 – Fourteen Sources For Finding Temporary Jobs 33
8 – How To Find Temporary Jobs Close To Home 41
9 – Online Resources For Finding Temporary Work................ 43
10 – Five Ways to Promote/Market Your Services................... 45
11 – How Much To Charge 55
12 – How To Earn $20,000 To $200,000 Annually 61
13 – Receiving Messages 67
14 – Accepting An Assignment 71
15 – Parking 73
16 – Insurance 75
17 – Advertising 77
18 – Dealing With Large Companies 79
19 – Getting Paid On Time 83
20 – Handling Bad Checks And No Pays 87
21 – Multiple Streams Of Income 91
22 – Five Simple Keys To Generate Repeat Business 93
23 – What If A Company Wants To Cancel without Notice?... 99
24 – Finding Work To Fill A Free Week 101
25 – Records To Keep 105
26 – Uncle Sam Wants His Share 107
27 – Conquer Your Fears 113

ACKNOWLEDGMENTS

A hearty "Thank you!" to the following people: Elisa Pacht, Rachel Norrod, Bob Woodburn, Melanie Stiles, John Sash, Wendy Walters and Stephanie and Ken Mays.

INTRODUCTION
WHY I BECAME A FREELANCE TEMPORARY

Having supervised two word-processing centers, I was frustrated with both jobs. One day a friend who was working in a law office mentioned that they needed a "temp" for about four months. They were going to pay the temp *more* money than I was making as a supervisor. I calculated that four months of pay at that rate would give me plenty of time for interviews so that I wouldn't have to rush into another permanent job. I quit my supervisory job and accepted the temporary position.

While on that first temporary assignment, at a friend's suggestion, I decided to try to do temporary work on a regular basis but wanted to find my own assignments. The frustration of "regular" jobs — finding them, and then dealing with the everyday mundane work — was so great that I decided I had nothing to lose. I reasoned that if I could earn at least as much money as I had been making previously on my regular job, it would be worth it. I had already seen that the money could be better. But it *was* scary, to say the least. I had visions of applying for food stamps after a month!

However, in my years as a Freelance Temporary, I earned excellent money and was still able to take off work more than *eight* and *nine* weeks each year! I discovered temp work *could* be steady. This book will tell you how.

Note: Although a Freelance Temp and contacts at companies may be male or female, I will generally use feminine gender for simplicity.

1
TEMPORARY WORK

Temp work can be steady, offer immense freedom, and provide good money — *if* you are your own agency, or what I call a "Freelance Temporary." Freelance Temps find their own work for temporary assignments, as opposed to going through traditional staffing agencies. I will be using the terms Freelance Temporary, Freelance Temp, freelancer, or freelancing for what they do. I will refer to temporary workers employed through a traditional agency as "agency temps." Your industry may call a temporary worker a contract employee. "Gig worker" is also a new catch phrase.

Any skill can be freelanced. My hairdresser mentioned how he could use a freelance stylist every now and then. Even professionals such as attorneys and engineers can freelance their work. Amazingly, surgeons can freelance: www.bit.ly/TempSurgeon.

The most common type of Freelance Temp, and the one I will emphasize, is a person who performs administrative or secretarial work. This book will provide the information you'll need to get started, build your client list, maintain good client relations, and work as often as you wish as a Freelance Temp.

Why Do Companies Employ Temp Help?

The four primary reasons industries hire temp help are:

1. A position has come open because an employee is temporarily absent due to vacation, sickness, hospitalization, maternity leave, or has taken a leave of absence.
2. The company has a vacancy and production must be maintained until a permanent employee is hired.
3. Seasonal work creates inconsistent workloads. For example, a law firm is going to trial with a big case, or an accounting business has end-of-year reports due.
4. The organization cannot afford - or does not want the expense of - providing the benefits they must pay a full-time employee.

Through both good and bad economic conditions, companies have consistently depended on temporary workers. However, a legal secretary recently reported that her employer had stopped using temps due to the current economy, forcing other employees to pick up the slack. If you encounter businesses that aren't hiring Freelance Temps, keep looking until you find those that are.

As a self-employed person, you will be paying for your own "benefits" (sick leave, health insurance, etc.). You'll want your income to be high enough to provide for those benefits, which also become deductions when tax time comes around. One of the greatest tax savings is a home office – but these will be covered later in this book.

Why Be a Temp, or Specifically, a Freelance Temp?

There are quite a few reasons.

Being a Freelance Temporary is *one of the best ways to find a good permanent position* if that is what you're ultimately looking for. Working as a Freelance Temp gives you a chance to get to know a company from the inside out. It also gives you the opportunity to show a company your excellent job skill. Doing so may allow you to start at a higher salary than someone the firm wasn't able to observe firsthand before hiring.

It has been speculated that after you're unemployed from one to two years, you are no longer considered a viable hire. Perhaps they fear that your job skills have become rusty or outdated. But working as a Freelance Temporary *keeps you in the job market, allows you to maintain your skills, and helps you to stay up to date with changes in your industry.*

Being a temporary worker offers the following advantages:
- It lets you earn income while searching for a permanent job.
- Gives you *great freedom and flexibility* in your schedule. Do you want time off during the summer with your kids? Want to vacation with your spouse when he can schedule time off? Or maybe, as a stay-at-home mom, you just want to get out of the house one week out of the month.
- Maybe you only want to work one or two weeks out of the month. This provides Baby Boomers, retirees and stay-at-home moms a good option.
- Can take the hassle out of having to go to work every day — and lets you avoid office politics.
- Can provide a good income.
- Can introduce you to a greater variety of work - as well as the opportunity to meet many types of people, since you will probably work for different kinds of companies, staffed by different workforces.
- Is an excellent avenue of re-entering the job market, as it helps you determine and develop the skills you have, and enables you to build on those skills.
- Can be a good source of income until you enter your desired career field. For example, I have talked to two authors who freelance. Often their assignments are not very demanding, with considerable idle time, affording them the option of working on their writing while on the job.

- If you are not sure which field you want to work in, being a Freelance Temporary lets you get a good feel for various fields - oil and gas, legal, real estate, engineering, accounting, etc.
- If you are single, working temp can put you in a professional environment and gives you a chance to meet other single people. Use extreme wisdom and caution here!
- Provides a fresh chance to market other services or products you would like to promote. Do you make jewelry as a hobby? Do you offer computer consulting in addition to your primary service? Being a Freelance Temporary puts you in new offices on a regular basis, giving you the chance to build trust and eventually promote your auxiliary services/products. This is discussed in detail in Chapter 21.

Why Freelance as Opposed to Working Through a Traditional Staffing Agency?

By freelancing, you show you are confident in your skills. A person without good skills wouldn't likely have the confidence for freelancing.

A Freelance Temp may well provide superior service compared to an agency temp. A Freelance Temp *must* care about her work because repeat business is vital to her survival.

A Freelance Temp has the satisfaction of working for herself. You represent your own company, not some other business or agency in which you have no vested interest.

Being a Freelance Temp builds *your* reputation, not that of an agency.

Being a Freelance Temp allows you to start *your own company* with minimal capital outlay, increased tax benefits, and with little or no overhead (fixed business expenses, renting office space, equipment and other business expenses).

Constant, positive feedback and appreciation for your

services is common in freelancing and gives you excitement and satisfaction, coupled with the knowledge that you are providing a much-needed service to a company. Your successes build further confidence and encourage the risk-taking necessary for being a successful Freelance Temp.

Freelancing lets you deal directly with an establishment. Without an agency as a middleman, you'll know what kind of assignment you're getting into - and employers will know what kind of worker they're getting.

Most importantly: being a Freelance Temporary lets *you* take home *all* the money that you earn, instead of an agency getting 25% to 50% of what *you* have earned. Yes, their percentage is that high.

2
Your Company Name

Every Freelance Temp should have her own "company" name. Not only is it exciting to have an official moniker, but it can also be helpful in describing your services. At one time, I used *Word Processing Services*, which is more or less a general name. When I first started my company, I thought I might eventually develop a consulting business, so didn't want to limit my options by including the word "temporary." I have since changed my company name, as I am no longer considering the consulting option.

Why Use a Company Name?

There are several advantages to using a company name.

A company name can help your temporary employer, as most groups prefer making out a check to a company, as opposed to an individual. That way, if the organization is audited, the check simply will reflect payment to a company. But if their check is made out to an individual, questions might possibly arise: Should this person be on payroll? Did they send the individual a 1099-Misc. form at the end of the year? Was all paperwork completed thoroughly and correctly? Such questions could potentially result in additional paperwork for their staff, which obviously is not something they want. You should streamline payment as much as possible, and by having your check made out to a company name, questions wouldn't be raised any more than if an auditor were to come across a check made out to Kelly Services.

Always be prepared to give all companies a W-9 form.

Using a company name, along with a business card, gives you a more professional image. It also makes you *feel* more professional psychologically.

Using a company name gives your clients confidence that you're a serious businessperson, not a fly-by-night operation.

Using a company name imparts the pride of "owning your own company."

Using a company name supplies a means of projecting a particular image. You can use a business name that includes your name (Patricia's Temporary Services). Or the name can suggest a specific service (Temporary Administrative Services). When trying to think of your company name, pass the word around to your friends and green-light ideas with them. Have a "Name My Company" party. Doing so will not only help you find a great name, but also will give you the chance to ask for their help in spreading the word about, and getting referrals for, your new service.

Once you decide on your company name, you will next decide on your "job title." Most documents (credit applications, tax forms, etc.) request a job title. Here's your chance to have the title you've always wanted. Obviously, make certain it's accurate and not misleading.

Using a Company Name or "d/b/a" (Doing Business As)

Check with your County Clerk to see if you are required to register a company name in your county. In some counties, an individual who operates under any name other than her given name is required to register that "assumed" name as a "d/b/a," or Doing Business As. The registration fee may be as little as $10 to $15. Some clerk's offices charge an additional fee for the form to be notarized. You may know a notary public, personally, who can provide that service free of charge, saving you the fee. Your bank may provide this service for free also.

The easiest way to find out your county's requirements is to perform an internet search for "assumed name" fee and "[your] county, [your state]" or "[your county] clerk, [your state]." For example, "Harris County Clerk, Texas." Many county websites show the fees and allow you to print out the application from online. Fill out the form and have your friend notarize it before you go to the County Clerk's office to file it.

However, if you live in a rural county, sometimes a simple phone call to the County Clerk can answer your questions quickly.

Even if your county doesn't require registration, it's actually to your advantage to do so. Registering the name protects it, so no one else can work under that name - only you. After you register, the county will list you with an official d/b/a.

In addition to counties requiring registration, some states require both corporations and individuals to register a d/b/a with the Secretary of State's office. Check with your Secretary of State's office for its requirements using the search information above but substituting "[your state's] secretary of state" for "[your] county."

Please note: You do *NOT* have to wait until you file your assumed name to use that name. However, your new designation will not be protected, and you will not be certain it's not already in use until you have registered it. Usually, you can check for duplications online - the County Clerk's office will show you how to perform the search when you register. Resist the urge to avoid this step. First, while this process may sound complicated, in reality, it's very simple. Second, you don't want to incur the expense of having your stationery and cards printed, only to find that your name has already been registered by someone else.

When you file your d/b/a at the County Clerk's office, you will be given an official sheet showing the county seal, your name, etc. Keep this in a safe place. You will need it for instances we will discuss later.

Should You Incorporate?

The main advantage of incorporation is for tax breaks; however, the primary tax advantages are in retirement and profit-sharing plans, which are essentially only of benefit to large companies. You can glean some of the same tax benefits through IRAs or 401(K)-type plans as a self-employed person without the added bother or expense of incorporating. Ask a knowledgeable tax accountant for advice.

Also, if you incorporate, you will have to pay corporate taxes in addition to your own income tax, meaning you'll be paying taxes on the same money twice.

Whether or not to incorporate goes far beyond the scope of this book. Consult an attorney or tax accountant to help you answer this question. We will discuss later the advantage of registering your d/b/a as a "Sole Practitioner/Proprietor."

DBA on a Checking Account

Many banks now offer free or at least low fee small business accounts that focus on the needs of small businesses. And, some banks will not deposit a check into your personal account if the check is made out to a company name.

When you are setting up a small business account, take the official d/b/a sheet from the County Clerk's office as proof that the company name is indeed representative of you.

I currently have a small business account because, as mentioned above in *Why Use a Company Name?* most companies prefer to make a check out using your company name. Banks will often require an account bearing that name in order to cash or deposit that check. Some banks will allow you to simply add your company name on your personal account. Just check with them and see what they require.

Business Stationery

When starting your business, you must have a business card. Again - business cards are a must! You will eventually need stationery to follow up with assignments and for contacting potential clients.

Always have business cards handy to give friends and any prospect you meet by appointment or by chance, or to send to prospects. Leave your card with people at your assignments. Especially those who find/hire their own temporary employees.

Unlike business cards, business stationery and envelopes are unnecessary when you're starting off. I didn't use any for about a year. However, you can present yourself in a more professional manner with a well-designed letterhead. Most printers will print envelopes to better present your follow-up letters. Don't worry, though. It isn't necessary to use an expensive letterhead and envelope. You can print your own if you have an eye for design and a good printer.

I currently get my business cards from www.Vistaprint.com. Sign up for their subscription emails because they often have good specials. Sometimes you can get "free" cards for the cost of postage, and they have a wide variety of templates from which to choose.

Options for your stationery include:
- Designing your own with verbiage and/or text only. Computers come equipped with an assortment of fonts, making it easy to do so. Letterhead can be as simple as your company name, address, etc., centered at the top of the page.
- Designing your own with verbiage and a logo. If you're artistic, by all means, design a unique logo for your company. Doing so can make your company stand out. Bear in mind, however, that you're striving for a

professional image, so keep it simple.
- Choosing a predesigned letterhead/card style. Most print companies, as well as office supply stores like Office Depot/Office Max, have large books from which you can pick a format and have them do all the work. Finally, websites such as Vistaprint offer many of their own options.

You will want your stationery to represent a professional picture of you. You do not have to have a logo or artwork for your letterhead and/or card to have it appear professional. You can simply have your name, address, phone number, etc., being sure to include a simply named email address. Never use an address such as: I_like_kittens@gmail.com or susiecutie@yahoo.com. Keeping it professional is best. And please have a good-sized font for your phone number, so that it is easily read.

I also recommend printing the items on off-white or lightly colored good-quality paper. On a desk with a sea of white letterhead, your off-white or lightly colored letterhead will stand out. Again, you want a professional look, so don't go to an extreme by using bright or gaudy colors.

Branding Your Marketing Materials

As you design your brand for your business, consider these points:
- Put your picture on your business card, flyer and any other marketing material. As you distribute these when you work in different places, anyone who sees your card will be reminded of who you are.
- Choose a special font style for your name and use that special font everywhere you put your name. Check out www.elements.envato.com. There is a nominal fee for this. You can enter your name and see how it looks with each font. Be sure each letter is easily readable, especially if you have an unusual name. Also, check out www.dafont.com.

Chapter 2 – Action Steps

1. Choose your company name and job title.
2. Register your company's assumed name with the County Clerk's office, setting it up as a d/b/a.
3. Establish your d/b/a with your bank. Have your checks printed with your company name for your company account.
4. Get a high-resolution photo to use on your business card and marketing material.
5. Pick out the font style for your branding material.
6. Order business cards and stationery or buy letterhead quality paper and envelopes.
7. Decide whether to incorporate and prepare your W-9 and tax forms accordingly.

3
PREPARING TO LAUNCH YOUR BUSINESS

Should You Start with an Agency?

I do *not* recommend this method.

You can start working temporary through an agency, which might help you feel a little more secure during any initial period of uncertainty. It will also afford you an opportunity to see if the "temp" field is for you. However, I only list it here because it's an option.

The process is too simple to not do it on your own. I *never* worked through an agency for any of my assignments. You *can* keep as busy as you'd like, without ever going through a traditional staffing agency.

You may already have a contract with an agency. The contract may state that, for a certain length of time, you cannot solicit any company's business if you found that company's work through their agency (unless you or the company for which you work pay the agency a fee). This length of time can be anywhere from three months to two years. However, there may not be any time limit at all. Your "contract" may only be what is on the back of your timecard or the "terms and conditions" you agreed to when you signed up with them online.

Honor any agency contract you may have. As a Freelance Temp, you'll be building your own reputation. You don't want to start off by contacting companies before your contract terms are up. This would indicate you are not one to honor a contract. You don't want to start your business with a lack of integrity.

My suggestion is not to get yourself into those contracts to begin with. *Again:* you do not need an agency!

Also, note that some agencies are regulated by state policy. For example, the agencies that place home healthcare workers are regulated. While you can, of course, work as a home healthcare Freelance Temp, you cannot represent yourself as a home healthcare agency, unless you're registered as required by your state.

The point: Be certain of your industry requirements before you call yourself an "agency" for that industry.

It's important to know that in order to cease working with an agency, all you have to do is stop accepting assignments. You don't have to offer any explanation or tell them you're freelancing, unless you specifically want to or you have agreed to notify them per any contract you agreed to. You should honor any sort of agreement in full.

What Service Will You Offer?

Summarize your previous work experience and examine how it all fits together. List each area of expertise. Do you have a real estate license and legal secretarial experience? If so, you have the ideal combination to be a Freelance Temp for a real estate attorney. Bring your skills together and promote your service to the people who need your combination of proficiencies.

I must emphasize: There is a vast choice of areas in which a person can freelance.

The following positions provide ideal opportunities for a Freelance Temp:
- Nurse
- Substitute schoolteacher
- Retail store clerk

- Cashier
- Surgeon
- Graphic artist
- Engineer
- Accounting clerk
- Welder
- Telephone/switchboard operator (especially if you know some of the sophisticated systems commonly in use)
- Daycare center worker
- Restaurant server
- Computer programmer/operator
- Auto mechanic
- Draftsman
- And, of course, administrative assistant

A variety of areas were listed to make a point - ANY SKILL CAN BE FREELANCED!

Yes, you're now self-employed! You are your own supervisor! How exciting!

Below is the two-pronged answer to my most often-asked question: "What should I do first?"

1. Decide what service you're going to offer; and,
2. Focus on who needs that service.

Prepare a Résumé or Promotional Flyer and Cover Letter

You will use a résumé or promotional flyer to promote your service. Preparing these documents will facilitate taking inventory of your skills and deciding what services you'll offer.

When writing your résumé, you do not have to list all of the companies for which you have been a Freelance Temp. You don't want to give away your client list. Just use the following format:

Freelance Temporary   January 1, 2017 to present

The date represents when you started working as a Freelance Temp. Even if you have worked at many different companies, you may use this format.

It would be an added expense, but if you don't feel confident composing your own promotional pieces, paying for assistance at a website like www.elance.com or www.fiverr.com may well be worth the investment.

Finally, create an effective cover letter using action verbs and a positive message about what *you* can do for *that particular company*. You'll use this correspondence as an introduction when forwarding your résumé or flyer.

Letters of Recommendation

As you serve different clients, ask for letters of recommendation. Use your best judgment as to when to use them, but certainly do so when one is requested, or if one of the letters is from a person or a company particularly meaningful to your new prospect.

Calendar/Appointment Book

You'll immediately need some type of calendar or appointment book to keep track of all those assignments you'll be getting!

Calendar options include:
- Your iPhone or Android
- Microsoft Outlook
- Google or Yahoo calendar

There are numerous calendar software choices available. Just be sure to back up any computer system regularly. Use a system you can have at your fingertips when a company calls to schedule your services.

You may get assignments up to six months in advance, so you certainly should write them on your calendar or log them in some appropriate manner as you get them. You could try a simple wall calendar or one of the accessorized planners available in office supply stores. Buy whatever you'll be comfortable with and will actually use.

Incidentally, I also use my calendar book to keep records of my smaller expenses, such as parking fees. We will discuss keeping records in detail later.

Should You Start with a Long-Term Assignment?

Initially, you may want to start with a long-term temp assignment, one for a length of about three or four months.

Taking an assignment of this length might help you mentally make the adjustment of not going to the same company every day, as when you had a permanent job. A three-to-four-month post will also help you get used to the idea of moving around and developing the flexibility you'll need as a Freelance Temp.

However, you may not have any control over the length of your first assignment, unless you *purposely wait* for a long-term assignment.

You may also want to consider the time of year you are beginning your freelance business. Is it a slow time for businesses, such as Christmas or year-end? Launching your company when commerce is intrinsically sluggish could be discouraging. You might feel as though it's only your company going through a tough run, when it's really an industry-wide issue. Try to find out when the best time for Freelance Temporary work is for your field. For administrative work, summer is usually the busiest for me.

State Requirements

Check with your State Department of Labor and Standards to see if you, working as a self-employed business owner, will need to be licensed with your state or county. Some states do not require licensing, especially if you're the only person working through your agency. In Texas, only permanent placement agencies are required to be registered and its employees licensed, while a temp service is not required to be registered. These regulations are things you need to keep in mind if you intend to get into the permanent placement end of this business.

Membership in a Professional Association

It will be helpful for you to become a member of one or more professional associations related to your areas of concentration. Most associations allow "vendor" memberships, or memberships for service and supply companies associated with their group. A vendor membership may save money on association fees.

Membership advantages include:
- An opportunity to keep current with changes in your industry, as well as an exchange of ideas with others in your area of expertise.
- The chance to build expertise in your field, thus enhancing the image you project to your clients.
- The association information on your stationery and cards, setting you apart from many other workers and demonstrating your seriousness and commitment.
- Networking opportunities - contact with people who need your service!
- The possibility of a health insurance plan with a group rate, or at a better rate than you might otherwise would receive.

Check the *Encyclopedia of Associations* at your local library for listings of associations connected to your skill set; or search the internet for other sources, including the National Association for the Self-Employed at www.nase.org.

Start-up Costs

How much will all of this cost? Investment expenses vary and depend on how elaborate you choose to get (engraved or commercially printed stationery, as opposed to printing your own at home; buying a sophisticated planner, as opposed to using a wall calendar). The estimates listed here are based on figures at the time of publication. You can start your company very economically according to *how* you want to start, as well as your available financial resources.

Estimates of individual start-up costs are as follows:

- Registering your d/b/a: approximately $10 to $15.
- Receiving messages (discussed in detail in Chapter 13): depends entirely on your chosen method of message reception. Most people use a cell phone, which can cost anywhere from $25 to $150 per month, with an initial cost, depending on current offers, plans, usage and phone expense.
- Printing: minimal if you simply use your computer. Expenses in this category can include the cost of hiring a graphic artist, unless you choose a pre-designed letterhead style or design your own; the cost of producing your cards; the cost of letterhead paper and envelopes; and the cost of having your résumé or promotional flyer printed, or perhaps have a service with which you can barter for your printing. You might even ask if you can be a Freelance Temp in exchange for the stationery. Also, Vistaprint options are very economical when you use their discounts.
- Appointment Book: A Month-at-a-Glance planner is approximately $17. Many computers come equipped with Microsoft Outlook®. Check out these options: http://www.printablecalendar.ca/, or perform a Google search. Common choices would be the calendar on your iPhone or using Google calendar.
- Postage: should be minimal, as you'll primarily be calling people and building a list of email contacts. However, ALWAYS follow up each call with a posted letter or email.

- Professional association dues: this depends on how many you join, as well as each association's fees.
- Advertising: *zero, if you use the methods in this book.* Add the fee for any advertising you wish to try.
- Credit reports or background checks: free, as these are readily available online through the three major credit reporting agencies (TransUnion, Experian, and Equifax). If a company runs any of these inquiries on you, feel free to ask for a copy. You can also check these free resources: www.AnnualCreditReport.com and www.CreditKarma.com.
- Because there are many temporary jobs that require specialized tools (for example a window washer), I am not listing these costs. You will have to determine what tools you can get by without when you start your temp business to save on start-up expenses.

Guard against getting carried away.

You do not need a sophisticated computer, a huge private office, fancy filing cabinets, etc. Yes, these luxuries are nice. Just don't get bogged down in using your time and money to buy unnecessary equipment and supplies.

Focus on contacting clients.

So, let's see what an actual start-up expense sheet might look like (asterisked items are considered essential, not optional). Refer to the following table:

Start-Up Costs

	Minimum
Obtaining d/b/a	$14.00
Receiving messages	
Cell Phone or answering service	$____
Printing (Vistaprint offers free shipping)	
Cards - 250 minimum	$8.00
Résumé/Flyer - 50	_____
Printed Stationery/Envelopes -	_____
Package of bonded paper and envelopes -	_____
New checks	_____
Appointment Book (Outlook or Google calendar)	$0.00
File Folder	_____
Postage	$10.00
Professional Association	_____
Advertising	
Brochures	_____

From these estimates, your minimum start-up costs can be as low as $32.00. You can see that your total expenditure would depend largely on how extravagantly you decide to begin your business and are very subjective. It also depends on what type of business you have and the tools needed. I have provided figures for the bare minimum, but you can choose to go upscale, as well. *Remember:* All these expenses will be tax deductible, which we will discuss in Chapter 26.

Keep in mind there *is* a certain amount of *risk* involved, which we will address in detail in Chapter 27. However, there's risk involved in *any* worthwhile project. But if you offer good service and do your part to find leads, you can keep busy and earn good money.

Let's see how ...

Chapter 3 – Action Steps

1. List all previous work experience.
2. While putting this list together, determine what type of temporary service you're going to offer. What service do you *want* to offer?
3. Update your résumé and/or promotional flyer.
4. Obtain letters of recommendation.
5. Choose your mode of receiving messages and implement immediately.
6. Establish your calendar method - Outlook, phone calendar, Google calendar?
7. Obtain a file folder to hold your records, such as copies of invoices and correspondence.
8. Establish a method of keeping tax receipts together, whether it's using an expense book or a pouch designated specifically as a receipt-holder or a phone app like Taxbot.

4
SHOULD YOU HAVE A WEBSITE AND FACEBOOK PAGE?

Take a deep breath. Creating a website is not as complicated as you might think. If you already have experience with web development, you're ahead of the game. But if not, you still have good options.

I have already mentioned Vistaprint in the segment on printing your résumé and promotional flyers. Fortunately, they also have a section for building websites. I've had a website through them before, and they made it easy for me to put it together. I would even go so far as to say it was fun.

Consider the following websites for hosting or web building:
www.bluehost.com
www.siteground.com
www.squarespace.com
www.hostgate.com
www.wix.com
www.godaddy.com
www.wordpress.com

These websites offer many template designs from which to choose and then provide tutorials on how to plug in your specific information.

What is the number one thing you want someone to do when they visit your website? Call you for an assignment. Make your phone number large and obvious. Don't make people click through several pages trying to find your phone number!

A business Facebook page is a relatively simple way to have an online presence. Post things on a regular basis regarding your industry.

See, that wasn't so bad. Don't get carried away with bells and whistles that won't significantly advance your business. Yes, it would be great to have a website and Facebook page, but do not get bogged down with this. It isn't necessary to get started.

Chapter 4 – Action Steps

1. Decide which website company you will use.
2. Have fun choosing your webpage template.
3. Set up your Facebook business page.
4. Don't get bogged down with this. Keep it simple. This doesn't have to be complicated.

5
UPDATING YOUR SOFTWARE SKILLS

With the continuing development of new computer software and software updates, a person with current experience in any type of software can easily locate and maintain employment. The more programs/equipment you can efficiently operate, the broader your client base can be.

How does a person gain experience with software or any special office equipment? Try these tips:
- If you are presently working for a company, check to see if they have any special equipment or software. If so:
  - Ask if they will send you to training classes to learn how to operate it;
  - Ask someone in the office to teach you; or
  - Find the manual or teaching program/disc for the equipment's software (or get a book or disc from the library) and teach yourself. Many programs come with a tutorial disk.
- Sign up for a class at a training center that focuses specifically on developing software skills. Course rates vary greatly depending on the thoroughness of the training. If you go this route, be sure you're training on software for which there is a large demand. Two of the main computer programs currently being used are Microsoft Office® (Word, Excel, etc.) and WordPerfect®/Corel® (in the legal

field). WordPerfect is in much less demand, but gives you an advantage if you can offer that skill also. Windows® programs are always very popular. Read the want ads. What skills appear to be in greatest demand in your area?
- Check for YouTube tutorials.

I believe it is worthwhile to obtain special training in several different software applications, as that field has been one of the fastest growing demands in the business world for many years. Need some motivation to get training? Learning as many programs as possible is an excellent way to set yourself apart from other temps.

If you do decide to take formal training through a commercial school, don't be timid about asking for the instructors' qualifications. How long has he/she worked with the equipment or program? How long has he/she taught the class? Does he/she have any special certifications?

- Investigate these other training opportunities:
    - Video training programs like Video Professor. Search "Video Professor" and "TeachUcomp" on eBay, and you'll see those and similar programs available for purchase. They are a very good value.
    - Your local community college. Research the curriculum, as not all of these schools specialize in computer or business training. Talk with a guidance counselor about your needs.
    - State unemployment commissions. Some of these offices provide free software training, so it would probably be worthwhile for you to call your local bureau and see what they offer. One unemployment office in Texas at one time gave access codes to use on www.proveit.com.
    - Friends. One commonly overlooked source of

information is your own friend base. Is there someone you know who works on special equipment or with a particular program you want to learn? Would they be willing to teach you?

- Locate a company that owns the equipment or software you're interested in. Offer to do a certain amount of work for free in exchange for allowing you to sit at one of their computers and train yourself using the training manual or video. Obviously, you'll need to establish some credibility with this company before making such a request.
- Use a referral and/or recommendation from a friend who works at a company that owns the equipment or software.

Use caution while self-training, unless you have had previous experience with similar equipment/software. Concepts and theory are vital and are best gleaned in a formal training class environment. Even if you know one software program, it's not true "if you know one, you know them all." The concepts may be similar, but you cannot necessarily be familiar with one program, then sit down at a different one and be in immediate production. Catching up on software updates always takes some adaptation time.

I do not recommend that you accept a temp position under such circumstances. *Be ready to give FULL, COMPLETE and EFFICIENT service for ANY Freelance Temp position you accept.*

I would recommend accepting an assignment for which you have little experience ONLY if the company fully understands your limited familiarity. If you've proven yourself, they may see you as a quick learner and be willing to use you, in spite of your limited know-how. But always be up front and honest about your level of skill and understanding.

If you have some down time, while on a Freelance Temp assignment, and there's new equipment or software in the office, ask to work on it so that you might learn its operation on your own.

Doing so will give you training and experience, not to mention increased value to your client.

There are advantages to offering both a specialty service and a general administrative service. With a specialty, you may be able to charge a slightly higher rate, but your area of potential clients will be limited. A Freelance Temp with good basic skills can get business from any company.

It's just a matter of finding the people who need the service *you* have to offer and marketing your service to those people.

REMEMBER: ANY SKILL CAN BE FREELANCED

Chapter 5 - Action Steps

1. Research what software may be new, but popular, in your field and take steps to update your skills as much as possible. Online training? Training DVDs available on eBay?

6
START YOUR CLIENT LIST

Most companies eventually use temporary help; therefore, any company that uses a person with your particular skill set is a potential client for you.

Make a decision about how you will track your clients. A very simple starting point would be through Microsoft's Excel (or Libre's Calc or Google Sheets).

Use Outlook as your contact manager.

In Outlook, go to the Home Tab. On the far right click on "Address Book." In the pop-up box click "File." Click on "New Entry." You will want different categories to keep updated information on the contacts in each company. This software also offers the "Notes" section where you can enter the information below.

Let's examine the different areas of potential clients and the information you should have on each.

Your client list should include:
- Initial date of contact
- Contact source (see Chapter 7). Who or what contact source referred you to them?
- Initial contact name
- Contact's company name, address and phone number, including specific extension numbers of everyone you dealt with in the company

- Any other contact phone numbers, possibly direct line numbers, for different people
- Email addresses/website
- Any special equipment or software expertise the company requires

Every time you make a contact that seems like a good fit for your service, add them to your client list database.

And, every time you work at a company, update the information on your client list that includes personal information. Don't trust your memory! Write it down. The more you remember, the more the office will respond to you favorably. For example, do you recall children's names? Someone's hobby? It's possible you'll return to a company a year or two later, and it would be impressive, to everyone involved, if you could go back knowing people's names. In today's impersonal world, people love to be remembered, so accomplishing that feat would be an undeniable plus. When you contact the company later and ask for specific individuals, they'll see you as an organized professional. Your goal is to be the first one they call, so consider no information about the employees as trivial.

Chapter 6 - Action Steps

1. Decide which contact management system you will use.
2. Immediately, when you find a company that could use your services, add them to your client list.

7
FOURTEEN SOURCES FOR FINDING TEMPORARY JOBS

So, what are some sources for companies to add to your client list?

1. Your Current Workplace

If you're currently employed in a full-time position and decide to begin working as a Freelance Temp, advise your employer of your plan – when the time is right, of course.

That company knows the quality of your work. They know you're familiar with their routines and procedures. Having that knowledge may lead them to prefer that you do their temp work, rather than take chances on someone new. After all, you represent a savings to them in terms of training and familiarization of office structure and personalities. There is nothing more comfortable than a perfect fit.

Once, when calling companies to seek a new temp assignment where I'd previously worked as a Freelance Temp, an office manager told me that very thing. One of their employees had quit her full-time position at the organization but had since been cross-trained to fill any of their temp positions.

What is one of the most important things you can do as soon as you begin any job? Network! Even when working at a company you know you may soon be leaving.

Hand your business card to everyone in the company.

Business cards are relatively inexpensive, so give them freely. You may never know "the contact" that will refer you for another assignment.

2. Your Previous Workplace

Again, if you left a company on good terms, they will generally be pleased to use you as a temp worker because they know you and your work. Contact any company you have worked for and let them know you're looking for Freelance Temp work. Then follow up by sending them one of your business cards. Ask for current email addresses.

Include any company you have worked for through temporary staffing agencies. Again, honor any contract you had with the agency and do not contact these companies until your contract obligation not to compete (the non-compete clause) has expired. The usual contract states one year, but the time frame can vary.

A company that hired you through an agency probably also has a contract with the agency, stating the same stipulation. You would be putting them in a difficult position by calling prior to the end of that time and essentially asking them to break their contract. Instead, contact these companies as soon as that phase is up. Let them know you're working on your own as a Freelance Temp. Then send them one of your business cards.

Another approach is to call your prior company and ask for referrals to *other* companies, as it is doubtful your contract would prevent you from doing that!

3. Where you *want* to work.

Has it always been your dream to work for Shell Oil Company? Check their website. Contact their Human Resources department. Companies sometimes list jobs, including temporary jobs, on their website.

4. Friends – Post on Facebook/Social Media!

I gained one of my best clients through a friend's referral. Friends can be a very good source of leads. Let them all know you're going to start working as a Freelance Temp, then be liberal about passing out your business cards. Your friends *always* need to have some on hand, in case they run into someone who might be a potential contact for you.

After confirming that they wouldn't mind your using them as a reference, ask your friends for the names and numbers of their personnel director, or hiring manager, or whoever schedules/hires the temporary help. Usually, they'll be glad to deliver one of your cards to the correct person or support you in any way possible.

Simply ask your friends if they are willing to support you in this way. Give them a list of options on *how* they can support you in your new business.

Call and establish contact with these associates. Send them one of your business cards if your friend hasn't already taken one to them.

Post on Facebook and let everyone know about your new business venture. Post your business card and promotional flyer. Maybe even send a private message to each friend who could be a local source for you.

If you're new in a city, friend referrals are a great way to make new friends. After you introduce yourself in person, explain the kind of work you do and ask for a referral. You can even employ this same tactic after meeting your neighbors. Tell them you're new to the city and would love it if they could share any contacts that might be helpful in your quest for Freelance Temp work.

5. The Newspaper

Though some major newspapers have closed down, those that remain are still good sources. The classified section in your local newspaper lists many companies looking for permanent employees.

Even if you're not seeking full-time employment, call them or contact them by the means they have requested. Explain that you're *not* looking for a permanent position, but that you do Freelance Temp work. Ask if they need temp help until they hire someone for the advertised position. I have found work this way!

This holds true if you ARE looking for a permanent position. Call and offer to work on a temp-to-hire basis.

Even if a company already has a temp, they may have you come in. I once called a company, and though they had hired a temp from a local agency, she could not adequately do the work. So, they let that temp go and hired me!

If you see an ad for the particular service you offer (e.g., Microsoft experience, legal assistant), be certain to send them a letter and a business card. Freelance Temps get leads from ads, and I landed one of my jobs in this manner.

6. Your Specialty Company

If you're offering a temporary "PBX Operator" service, call several companies selling the phone system with which you're proficient and speak with a salesperson. Explain what you're doing. Ask if any of their customers have needed temporary PBX Operators for that specific system. If so, request the referrals. Contact each company they note and send them a business card with a cover letter.

Also, follow up with these salespeople and send them your business cards and a handwritten note.

7. Referrals

When you work for a company, ask the following of every person you get to know:

- Does she know of another company in the building that

could use your services?
- Would she be amenable to your using her as a reference?
- Would she refer you to her friends who are working at other companies?

8. Business Network Groups

Business network groups usually advertise in local business papers and include groups like www.bni.com, which has an annual fee. Check for local meet-up groups at www.meetup.com for your city. Another option, a Facebook group for your industry/service.

9. Craigslist

While looking for work, *daily* search your city's craigslist (www.craigslist.org). Contact every company that appears as though it would be a good fit for you. Advertisers on craigslist usually only operate digitally, so you'll want to email your résumé and cover letter. If you don't receive an email or call in response, reply to the craigslist ad again, even up to three times.

Be cautious with Craigslist and be sure you are dealing with a legitimate company. Also, be aware that some of the ads are listings by employment agencies.

Respond in the way that they request, whether through a form they post, by email or by phone.

It will be greatly to your advantage to become familiar with a phone app called iTranslate. If an ad requests a bilingual person, and you are not bilingual in the language they are seeking, let them know that, but emphasize that you are very familiar with the iTranslate app which works with over 100 different languages.

Later we'll discuss using Craigslist to post ads promoting your service.

10. Optimize Your LinkedIn Account.

Update your LinkedIn profile and keep it current. Google "optimize LinkedIn profile" for current ideas on how to bring better results for companies searching on LinkedIn.

11. Online Referrals

See Chapter 9 for a list of internet resources.

12. Temp Jobs Close to Home

See Chapter 8 for how to find temp jobs nearby.

13.   Facebook Business Pages

Search for companies in your industry who need your services. Message them through Facebook or any other contact information they provide. Join these groups, but be careful to follow their guidelines.

14.   Job Fairs and Career Days

Some churches offer a "Career Day" or job fair. Could this be an opportunity for you to register as a vendor? If the event consists solely of companies looking for employees, attend and ask who, in each company, hires temporary workers. Get specific names and follow up with those people. Hand out your business cards and/or flyers at these events.

Building Your Client List

By now, you have a list of potential clients. As mentioned earlier, always keep your list updated with your contacts correct addresses, phone numbers, and email addresses. Also take notes as to their letter styles, different procedures, particular software preferences, policies, etc. You'll constantly add contacts and information to this list and refer to it often. *Frequently save a backup copy!*

My client list consisted of 80 companies, though I only worked for about 40 of them. Considering that I kept busy for five years, the number seems quite low. One year I worked for 13 companies, and another year I worked for only 11 companies, six of which were repeat clients from previous years. It doesn't take as many contacts to maintain a profitable work schedule as you might think.

Your client list will be a tremendous asset when you're looking for work. Since you may not call a company even once within a period of six months to three years, coupled with the fact that employee turnaround is high in many companies, some of the people you previously worked with will no longer be there. Therefore, it's a good practice to ask for a specific person when you call, as doing so will provide a better lead-in – obviously, you've had contact with their company before. Keeping your client list current will help you accomplish these things.

Chapter 7 – Action Steps

1. What kind of company needs the services you're going to offer? Check with your local library to see if you can find a list of these kinds of companies.
2. Establish your contact management software system.
3. Check the city directory or Cole's Directory at your local library for leads or check the Criss Cross Directory. You can find these online, but for a fee. Your library may be able to give you access at their location for free.
4. Create a list of all companies for which you've worked.
5. Make a list of all of your friends. Call, email or message them through Facebook to tell them what you're doing. Ask them for the names of the persons who hire temporary help at their workplace. Ask if you can use

them as references. Let them know the options of how they can support you.
6. Become familiar with iTranslate.
7. Start checking your local newspaper want-ads for potential clients.
8. Initiate contact with any "specialty" company from which you can get leads.
9. Keep your client list up to date by maintaining records of all companies from which you generate a positive response and the contact person.
10. As you make a contact, create an entry in your client list database.

8
HOW TO FIND TEMPORARY JOBS CLOSE TO HOME

If you'd like to work in a particular area of your city, visit your local library and check these references:
www.referenceUSA.com
www.demographicsnow.com
www.crisscross.com

You will need a library card with a pin number to access the sites, but it is worth it! These resources will give you a lot of data about the companies near you.

These directories list all of the companies at any given street address. For example, if you'd like to work in the building at 3000 Richmond Avenue, you'd look up 3000 Richmond. The directory lists each suite number in the building, the name of the company at that suite, and the telephone number of that company.

Ideally, you would go to each suite, ask to speak to the person who hires the temporary help. Explain to that person the services you offer, being certain to leave a copy of your résumé/flyer and business card.

By visiting each suite in person, you'll tend to generate business in a central location. Though some Freelance Temps are concerned that going from suite to suite might be considered soliciting, which is often not allowed in buildings, it's not. You're simply looking for work. I've talked to Freelance Temps who've developed their client list in this way, and temp agencies occasionally use this strategy to gain new accounts. So, if someone asks if you're soliciting simply say, "No, I'm looking for contract work."

Though I highly recommend going to each office, you may not have time to do so. If not, call them all and follow the same instructions for in-person visits. We'll discuss this further in Chapter 10.

Chapter 8 – Action Steps

1. Check out the references, mentioned in this chapter, at your local library.
2. Always send a handwritten thank you note or letter to every person you speak with about your services. Be sure you have carefully noted the correct spelling of each person's name.

9
ONLINE RESOURCES FOR FINDING TEMPORARY WORK

The following are a few internet resources for Freelance Temps. These links were active at the time of publication.
- www.UpWork.com
- www.indeed.com
- www.monster.com
- www.craigslist.org
- www.SnagAJob.com
- www.LinkedIn.com
- www.ZipRecruiter.com
- www.guru.com (This one has a free basic membership and has other memberships for a price.)
- www.Flexjobs.com (Monthly membership $15-$50/month)
- www.Backdoorjobs.com
- www.simplyhired.com/local-jobs
- A good one for me is www.lawyers.com

Some websites also get into skill testing and many things related to finding a job.

Some websites get more specific (i.e., www.IHireLegal.com).

If you google "find a job," or "find contract jobs," there are plenty of websites to choose from. If you are considering working temporary on a permanent basis, you would be wise to become familiar with many of these websites.

Even though some of these websites are for permanent jobs, you can contact them about working temporary until they hire someone.

Does the association you are a member of offer job seeking or posting on their website? Association membership was discussed in Chapter 3.

Keep a list of websites where you post your information and always keep it updated.

Chapter 9 – Action Steps
1. List which internet resources will give you leads in your field of work.
2. Maintain a list of where you post your information. Always keep it current.

10
FIVE WAYS TO PROMOTE/MARKET YOUR SERVICES

You have your client list and are constantly adding new clients, maintaining contact with existing clients, and connecting with appropriate contacts while you're looking for work. Listed below are some ways to reach out to these clients.

Your Initial Contact

There are four key ways a prospect's initial contact can take place:
1. On the phone. This will be the method you'll use most often, and will be the most cost-effective.
2. Via a personal office visit. Though time consuming, it's also quite effective.
3. Through mailing your résumé/promotional flyer. This is a rather costly endeavor, since effectiveness of direct mail generally requires large mailings (hundreds or thousands) and may yield a seemingly small rate of return (2 to 3 percent is considered good).
4. From referrals. They call you!

The Phone Call

You've been to the library and have a particular location in which you'd like to build your business. Perhaps you have found potential clients in the want-ads. What should you say when you call them?

Here is a sample conversation:

Potential client: Good morning, ABC Company.

You: Good morning. My name is Mary GoGetter. I work as a Freelance Temporary _____. Does your company need temporary help this week?

It's as simple as that! You can also mention whom you were referred by:

"This is Patricia Barnes. I was referred to you by _____. I'm a Freelance Legal Assistant and am checking to see if you need any help this week."

If you are told they don't need help, ask to speak with the person who hires the temporary help. Explain to that individual what you do, and offer to send them your résumé/flyer and a card.

Be upbeat and cheerful. A smile comes across in your tone of voice, as do apprehension and nervousness. Be mindful of your disposition. And while I've suggested an opener, by all means, say something that feels natural to you. Another tip I've used for many years is to stand while I am speaking.

Remember: It's not always the Personnel or Human Resources Department that hires the temporary help. Sometimes an administrative assistant is responsible for finding her own replacement, and other times, the person whose admin will be absent has to find their own temporary help.

Therefore, do not automatically ask for Human Resources or the Personnel Department. Ask for the "person responsible for hiring temporary help." Personnel Departments are located in somewhat large businesses, and you may encounter companies with no Human Resource Department at all.

During your call, be positive about yourself and your skills, but of course don't over-sell or misrepresent yourself. It would be to your discredit to accept a temporary job and not be able to perform the duties. Unfortunately, bad references seem to travel faster than good ones.

Call when you are genuinely upbeat, cheerful and alert.

When making your calls, expect some "nos." Not everyone will need your services. Not everyone will want to hire a Freelance Temporary, but you must call until you find the ones who will. That is what this process is all about. Just keep calling and you WILL find someone who will hire a Freelance Temp.

Be polite when you receive a "no." You never know when that company's needs will change. Keep them on your client list for follow-up at a later date.

Rejection, especially if you are a beginning caller, will affect you. At first, you may take it personally. Some freelancers find this to be the hardest part. A friend of mine, in a phone sales job, had a supervisor who handed out phonebook pages whose numbers she was required to call - just to get accustomed to rejection.

Keep in mind that companies have many salespeople contacting them to buy equipment, offer services, etc., and may not always have the time or desire to speak to you. Be persistent and call at another time. You never know when you're going to catch them just at the right time - when they need a Freelance Temp.

I know it's a cliché, but persistence is the name of the game. Working for yourself requires self-motivation - that's precisely why it pays more.

Objections and Responses

There are several standard objections companies raise about hiring a Freelance Temporary. When someone gives you an objection, question them about it. Answer their objection.

Here are some common objections and the suggested responses.

OBJECTION	YOUR RESPONSE
We only work through agencies.	I work through my own temporary agency.
We have a list of agencies; and we only work through them	Will you add my agency to your list? One Freelancer asked the City of Houston that question, and they added her agency to their list.
The Agencies perform credit and background checks	I can provide a copy of my recent credit report and background check.
We don't want to have to worry about paying your taxes.	When you make out your check to my company name, it's the same as though you'd make a check out to Kelly Services. You don't have to take out taxes for them, and you don't for me. I pay quarterly estimated taxes. I will provide a W-9 if necessary.
We can't hire someone not covered by Workers' Compensation.	One company added me to their list of employees for whom they paid Workers' Comp. Information about Workers' Compensation is discussed later.
We have to have someone who's passed security clearance,	My agency [or I] will go through any clearance

which is usually done through the agency.

procedures you require.

If none of these responses work, ask them WHY they insist upon using an agency. They may repeat one of the objections above or come up with a new one.

FIND OUT THEIR OBJECTION AND ANSWER IT FOR THEM. RESOLVE THE PROBLEM.

You'll have to educate companies to the fact that making a check out to your company is exactly the same as making a check out to Kelly Services (or any other agency). In every way. Period. Again, be prepared to give them a W-9.

Help them understand that they would be simply dealing with a company like any other company they deal with on a daily basis. When they make out a check to Kelly Services, they don't have to worry about taxes. The same is true for your company.

In an effort to reassure them, you might offer to do any of the following:

- Provide a contract that both you and the company representative will sign. Search for a simple form online, check with an attorney or check with Office Depot/Max.
- Provide references; carrying a list of references and a letter of recommendation with you is good practice.
- Interview with the person you will be working for.
- Assure them of your experience and give them a résumé/promotional flyer.
- Let them know your company is registered with the County Clerk's office.

If a company seems unreceptive throughout the phone conversation, as a last resort, you may offer to send them one of your business cards in case the agencies aren't able to find someone for them at any given time. Even if they don't seem interested, follow up with a letter and business card and/or flyer.

If it is a very good assignment and long-term, even consider offering to work for free for a half-day or one day. I was recently in an office that received an email from Robert Half in which they were offering one day free.

You'll encounter some companies that simply will not work with a Freelance Temporary – only about 5% or less. Most companies will, however, and without any of the objections listed earlier. But when starting, you need to realize some companies will have objections simply because it's a new, unconventional idea.

Part of your job in promoting your services is to educate people to this type of solution for their temporary needs.

1. The Office Visit

Your approach for this method is much the same as for making a phone call, except this time you have a chance to present a real picture "in person." Presentation is important. Dress in a conservative manner, at least until you have a chance to observe office "dress code" or style in that particular environment. Make sure your nails and teeth are clean, and your hair is in place. This is your first impression, and, as they say, you'll never get a second chance to make a first impression.

Be prepared with your responses to any potential objections. It might be a good idea to practice before venturing out, or even making your phone calls. That way, you will sound more natural.

Your first task will be to convince the receptionist that you're worth "bothering" the person who hires temps. Here's where image decidedly comes into play. This is not the time to give in to your "free spirit," unless your industry lends itself to that.

Present the receptionist with your résumé/promotional flyer and card. Reassure her you are a Freelance Temp looking for work, not a solicitor or salesperson. Maintain good eye contact. Listen carefully to the words and notice the body language of the person you're talking to.

If, at this time, the receptionist objects with the "only through an agency" line, you can say you work through your own agency. Ask to speak to the person who hires the temporary help. Be patient and pleasant.

Office visits are a convenient way to promote your service while working in a particular building. Just drop by other suites in the building on your lunch break. Offer the company you're working for as a reference. Often, everyone is familiar with other businesses in the building, so using that company's name might help you to get your foot in the door. *Note:* This method takes much more time than using the telephone. So, try telephone contact first, unless you're already on assignment in the building.

Again, accept the fact that there will be objections and rejections. Keep your goals in focus. Consider objections as practice, because that's exactly what they are. Very good practice, at that!

2. The Mailing

You might also make initial contact through a marketing letter or mailing. Send mailings to the companies that need your particular service, or companies whose addresses you obtain from the City Directory.

With this method, you will incur the additional expenses of printing and postage, therefore, carefully monitor how many you send. For example, if you're going to need work in a couple of weeks, mail about 50 flyers. Or send out 10 to 20 flyers regularly each month. Soon you'll know how many it takes to generate the business you need.

3. The Referral

The referral takes place when a company calls you, the result of someone referring you from a previous job, or a friend who left your card at their office. On occasion, you may also receive referrals from your "special equipment" company, as well as responses from your advertisements or promotional flyers.

4. The "Contact Us" Online Form

You have found a business you want to work for. Go to the "Contact Us" link on the company website. Many companies now have an online form you can fill out to get in touch with them. Insert a short cover letter and copy your résumé into this form. I personally obtained a job interview this way.

5. The Follow-up Letter

ANY TIME, EVERY TIME, a company responds in a positive way, follow up with a letter and one of your cards, even if you've already left a card with them. Letters are more effective when addressed to a particular person and written in a personal manner with as much "you" in them as possible. Other options for follow-up are:

- Sending a handwritten thank you note or a postcard.
- Follow up via email.

It is not necessary or recommended to state your rate in your letter unless you are specifically asked to do so. If you state your rate, be sure to add "at this time, my rate is $___ per hour."

Don't bring up the subject of rates until they do, *unless* they've called, scheduled an assignment, and you've *still* not discussed it. This has happened to me. You do not want to show up for an assignment, and *then* find out they think your rate is too high.

As you receive positive responses and prepare your follow-up letters, add all company information to your growing client list. You'll be calling each of them from time to time.

Finally, there will be some companies who resist change at all costs and simply will not consider the idea of hiring a Freelance Temporary. It's a new idea they do not want to accept.

PART OF PROMOTING YOUR SERVICE IS EDUCATING COMPANIES ABOUT USING A FREELANCE TEMPORARY.

It is a relatively new alternative. Typically, the only thing a company knows to do when they need temporary help is to call a commercial staffing agency.

Make it Easy for People to Do What You Want Them to Do

If you want someone to call you – show your phone number very prominently on your website and/or business card. There is plenty of room on a business card for a good-sized phone number. I have often seen business cards where anyone would need a magnifying glass to see the number. Don't make them search through several web pages to find your phone number or email.

If you want someone to leave a review, give them a link. Don't say "go find me on Yelp." To insert a link to the review page, or your website:

Go up to the URL address area where you want them to go.

Right click on whatever is there in the URL, then choose "Copy."

Then go to where you are inserting it for them to see (Facebook comment, in an email, on your webpage, etc.)

Click Ctrl V. This will insert what you copied.

Chapter 10 – Action Steps

1. Begin calling everyone you've gotten a reference for. Explain what you're doing. Promote your services. Ask if

they currently need temporary help.
2. Follow up with a postcard, letter, or handwritten note, accompanied by one of your business cards.
3. Obtain letters of reference to have available when requested.
4. Set up a Facebook page for your company.
5. Become active on Linked-In.

11
How Much To Charge

Yet another vital decision in your new role as a self-employed individual, and one that requires serious consideration, is how much you should charge for your services.

Setting Your Rate

Your rate of payment will depend largely upon the rate established by agencies in your area. If a company can get a good temp through a traditional staffing agency for $35 an hour, they probably won't be willing to pay you more. However, let's assume your skills are equal to that of the top requirements in your category - you're a highly qualified legal assistant. If the agencies are charging $40 for a legal assistant, you could easily charge $25 or $30 per hour.

When you can demonstrate your experience, offer good references, and express confidence in yourself, companies will generally pay your rate. And, if you have top skills, you can price yourself at the top going rate. If you believe in your competency, so will management.

Be fair to the company, but also be fair to yourself.

How to Determine the Going Rate

It's not always easy to get information from agencies, especially when it concerns how much they charge companies to fill a particular temp position. Five ways you could obtain this information are by:

- Calling an agency on your current employer's behalf (if you're currently working).
- Asking any company you work for how much the agencies usually charge for the temp position you're filling. Most people usually don't mind giving you this information.
- Asking your friends to find out how much their companies pay agencies for temp help.
- Asking a friend to call an agency on behalf of the company they work for.
- Offering to do a research project on competitive rates for your current employer. Call the agencies, then present their numbers beside yours. Doing this will not only give you information on rates comparable for your position, but also let your company see how much money you're saving them with your rate.
- LinkedIn has a search feature where you can enter your job title and city and they will show the low, median and high salary for your location. This is a *great* resource. www.linkedin.com/salary.

That's what freelancing is all about - finding those companies who will use a Freelance Temporary, and finding the ones that will pay your rate. You might even be surprised to learn some companies may think you charge too little. You don't want to charge too *little* and have them wondering what might be wrong with your work.

Keep in mind: **THERE WILL ALWAYS BE A COMPANY THAT THINKS YOU CHARGE TOO MUCH.**

But also keep in mind: **THERE WILL ALWAYS BE A COMPANY THAT WILL PAY YOUR RATE!**

When I first started working as a Freelance Temp, I charged a very low rate. But one of my very first potential clients declared, "I'll let my computer sit there turned off before I'll pay that much!" I simply told him to call me if he changed his mind. Some basic guidelines for setting rates are:

- Charge as much as your level of confidence will allow you. You can probably get more than you think. You want your rate to be more than what an agency would pay you, but low enough to be competitive with the agencies.
- I do not charge an hourly rate, plus parking or mileage. It would be a reasonable expense to ask for if you feel you need to include both charges. This option is up to you. Your industry may dictate what is proper. Your cost for parking will be minimal if you follow the instructions in Chapter 15. Charge everyone the same rate. If your work is dramatically different, e.g., sometimes you answer phones, while other times you program computers part-time, you would obviously charge different rates for the different jobs. One Freelance Temp I heard of charges less when she works close to home. Again, this is a personal decision you will have to make. Just be sure to keep accurate records on your client list of whom you charged what rate!
- Should you state your rate as "negotiable?" You may generally end up with a lower rate when you negotiate, but some freelancers offer negotiable rates for long-term assignments. Before you allow a company to negotiate you to a lower rate for a long-term assignment, consider that you could be working on short-term assignments at a higher rate. My rate is not negotiable. However, the decision to negotiate is yours to make.

Should You Back Down on Your Rate?

Should you back down on your rate if a company tells you it's too high? As long as you've done your homework and aren't overcharging, I think you'll better maintain your dignity and integrity if you stick to your rate. Assure them you have researched the going rates for your service and that your rate is reasonable. There *are* companies that *will* pay your rate. Just keep looking.

If you are making calls, you should be consistently finding work. If you're in a financial crisis, then of course, you'll have to consider that factor when you decide whether or not to back down on your rate. I say just keep making the calls — you'll find that company willing to meet your price!

Give Yourself a Raise!

As far as giving yourself a raise (doesn't that sound great?!), when you find out the going rate is higher than what you're charging, you can comfortably raise your rate. Keep up with current rates by talking to other temps and using the tactics described earlier. Also, ask the companies you work for how much the agencies usually charge for your position.

Every time I have increased my rate, I've feared no one would ever use my services again. My fears were completely unjustified. To reiterate, if one company won't pay your rate, there IS another company that will. You just have to find it. Very few companies will refuse to pay your rate, unless it is excessive or you're unable to offer references or assurance of your experience.

When should you provide notification of your rate increase?

The *only* time to give out this information is when a company calls to hire you back for your services.

You should try to remember who has and has not been informed about your rate increase. Note this on your client list or Outlook contact. When a company calls again for your services, wait until you've made all the arrangements and simply say:

"At this time, my rate is $___ an hour", or "I believe my

rate has increased since I last talked to you. It's now $___ an hour."

It would be to your advantage to wait to announce your rate increase until a company has called you with a need. If they need you, it'll be easier for them to accept your new fee. There is no reason to notify any company of a rate increase before they need you. I've never had a company quit using me because I increased my rate.

Overtime Rates

I charge overtime rates. My overtime rate is time-and-one-half. A company usually pays its employees the same overtime rate, and my time is as valuable as anyone else's. My work is not my life, and thus isn't worth the sacrifice of my evenings and/or weekends at my regular rate. You may decide to charge your regular rate for your overtime pay. Again, the decision is up to you.

I charge overtime rates for weekend work, with a four-hour minimum. A company once requested that I work on the weekend, and after rearranging my schedule to accommodate theirs, then traveling all the way to their office, I ended up working only 45 minutes! I decided that would not happen again. So began the four-hour daily minimum.

When to Discuss Rates

Do not *ever* bring up the subject of rates. The *only* exception I make to this rule is when I have made all the arrangements with a company for an assignment, but my rate has still not been discussed. At that point I'll mention, "My rate is $___ per hour." I want to be sure I do not end up working a week and *then* finding out they consider my rate to be too high. After your rate is discussed, always follow-up with a confirmation email.

When Not to Discuss Rates

Other than in the scenario above, I do not recommend bringing up the subject of rates. Outgoing money is not a pleasant topic, so why should *you* bring it up? Always discuss your services, the assignment, etc., and assume your rate will be acceptable.

In your promotional flyer, you might want to state something like "I'm sure you'll find my rate competitive." If you have a flyer or résumé with your rate on it, you will have to have it reprinted when your rate increases. I don't put my rate on these.

Another reason NOT to state your rate on printed materials is that it looks tacky and unprofessional to mark through something on a flyer, card or stationery. Avoid mentioning your rate in print. It is not necessary.

I also do not bring up the subject of my overtime rate, until the company mentions their need for me to work overtime. If they ask me to work overtime, *at that time,* I tell them I can, but that I charge an overtime rate, which should be no surprise to them. If, while making arrangements to go in for an assignment, they mention that some overtime may be involved, I'll then tell them about my overtime rate.

If a company says they use Freelance Temps, but they only pay a lower hourly wage than your usual rate, leave your name and phone number. Then, if they call you and NEED your services, then, at that time, let them know what rate you'll be willing to accept for the assignment. The advantage will be yours because they are calling, and *they* need you.

Chapter 11 – Action Steps

1. Make a decision about what rate you will charge.

2. Follow-up any discussion about rate with a confirming email, if connected with an assignment.

12
HOW TO EARN $20,000
TO $200,000 ANNUALLY

Another way to set your rate is to figure out how much you want to earn in the coming year. Divide that amount by how many weeks you want to work (based on how many weeks you *don't* want to work!). Divide that result again by a 40-hour week.

For example, let's say you wanted to be off ten weeks (two and one-half months!) and earn $50,000 next year.

52 weeks per year - 10 weeks = 42 weeks

$50,000 ÷ 42 weeks = $1,190.48 per week (the amount you must earn)

$1,190.49 ÷ 40 hours per week = $29.76 per hour (the amount you must charge)

Of course, you can round the number up to an even number. Keep in mind that some of the 10 weeks' time above will include holiday time you'll naturally have off. For example, most companies will give employees two days for Thanksgiving, and for a Freelance Temp this will probably be unpaid time. Several of the weeks will be time *you* plan to take off. At the very minimum, allow yourself three weeks off for holidays and times you'll need to place calls to find work. Also, we're basing these numbers on a forty-hour week, which sometimes varies due to personal time off for doctor's appointments or other engagements. But the numbers will average out because some weeks you may work overtime.

On the following pages are charts to help you see how much you will need to charge while taking a certain number of weeks off.

Weeks Off	Total Yearly			
	$20,000	**$30,000**	**$40,000**	**$50,000**
3	$10.20	$15.31	$20.41	$25.51
4	$10.42	$15.63	$20.83	$26.04
5	$10.64	$15.96	$21.28	$26.60
6	$10.87	$16.30	$21.74	$27.17
7	$11.11	$16.67	$22.22	$27.78
8	$11.36	$17.05	$22.73	$28.41
9	$11.63	$17.44	$23.26	$29.07
10	$11.90	$17.86	$23.81	$29.76
11	$12.20	$18.29	$24.39	$30.49
12	$12.50	$18.75	$25.00	$31.25
13	$12.82	$19.23	$25.64	$32.05
14	$13.16	$19.74	$26.32	$32.89
15	$13.51	$20.27	$27.03	$33.78
16	$13.89	$20.83	$27.78	$34.72

Weeks Off	Total Yearly			
	$60,000	$70,000	$80,000	$90,000
3	$30.61	$35.71	$40.82	$45.92
4	$31.25	$36.46	$41.67	$46.88
5	$31.91	$37.23	$42.55	$47.87
6	$32.61	$38.04	$43.48	$48.91
7	$33.33	$38.89	$44.44	$50.00
8	$34.09	$39.77	$45.45	$51.14
9	$34.88	$40.70	$46.51	$52.33
10	$35.71	$41.67	$47.62	$53.57
11	$36.59	$42.68	$48.78	$54.88
12	$37.50	$43.75	$50.00	$56.25
13	$38.46	$44.87	$51.28	$57.69
14	$39.47	$46.05	$52.63	$59.21
15	$40.54	$47.30	$54.05	$60.81
16	$41.67	$48.61	$55.56	$62.50

Weeks Off	Total Yearly			
	$100,000	$110,00	$120,000	$130,000
3	$51.02	$56.12	$61.22	$66.33
4	$52.08	$57.29	$62.50	$67.71
5	$53.19	$58.51	$63.83	$69.15
6	$54.35	$59.78	$65.22	$70.65
7	$55.56	$61.11	$66.67	$72.22
8	$56.82	$62.50	$68.18	$73.86
9	$58.14	$63.95	$69.77	$75.58
10	$59.52	$65.48	$71.43	$77.38
11	$60.98	$67.07	$73.17	$79.27
12	$62.50	$68.75	$75.00	$81.25
13	$64.10	$70.51	$76.92	$83.33
14	$65.79	$72.37	$78.95	$85.53
15	$67.57	$74.32	$81.08	$87.84
16	$69.44	$76.39	$83.33	$90.28

Weeks Off	Total Yearly			
	$140,000	$150,000	$160,000	$170,000
3	$71.43	$76.53	$81.63	$86.73
4	$72.92	$78.13	$83.33	$88.54
5	$74.47	$79.79	$85.11	$90.43
6	$76.09	$81.52	$86.96	$92.39
7	$77.78	$83.33	$88.89	$94.44
8	$79.55	$85.23	$90.91	$96.59
9	$81.40	$87.21	$93.02	$98.84
10	$83.33	$89.29	$95.24	$101.19
11	$85.37	$91.46	$97.56	$103.66
12	$87.50	$93.75	$100.00	$106.25
13	$89.74	$96.15	$102.56	$108.97
14	$92.11	$98.68	$105.26	$111.84
15	$94.59	$101.35	$108.11	$114.86
16	$97.22	$104.17	$111.11	$118.06

Weeks Off	Total Yearly		
	$180,000	$190,000	$200,000
3	$91.84	$96.94	$102.04
4	$93.75	$98.96	$104.17
5	$95.74	$101.06	$106.38
6	$97.83	$103.26	$108.70
7	$100.00	$105.56	$111.11
8	$102.27	$107.95	$113.64
9	$104.65	$110.47	$116.28
10	$107.14	$113.10	$119.05
11	$109.76	$115.85	$121.95
12	$112.50	$118.75	$125.00
13	$115.38	$121.79	$128.21
14	$118.42	$125.00	$131.58
15	$121.62	$128.38	$135.14
16	$125.00	$131.94	$138.89

Keep in mind the typical office worker generally gets two weeks of sick leave, two weeks for vacation, plus eight to ten paid holidays. However, this "typical worker" only gets sick leave if actually sick; otherwise, they lose that time. Obviously, you must have skills to match your rate. Besides that caveat, everything goes back to promoting yourself, making your calls, and providing a good service.

13
RECEIVING MESSAGES

You *must* have some way for your clients to contact you and/or leave a message for you — *and the sooner the better!*

A potential client will not wait two or three days to catch you on the phone or wait for you to return a call. They will contact other professionals, if they can't reach you.

THE ABILITY OF YOUR CLIENTS TO CONTACT YOU QUICKLY OR LEAVE A MESSAGE FOR YOU CAN MAKE OR BREAK YOUR BUSINESS.

Using a Cell Phone

Of course, this is the most common method. Using a cell phone for business calls means a good part of that bill is tax deductible.

Be sure to ask your current supervisor about any policies concerning cell phone use in your workplace. Some companies frown on using your cell phone on the job. Usually, the company will understand your need to be in contact with other clients, but more than likely prefer minimal phone usage for that purpose or any other. Use integrity and honor any policy they may have regarding cell phone usage.

Having Someone Answer Your Phone

Whoever answers your phone *must* be someone who is *always* available to do so, not just a friend who will be in and out or have screaming kids in the background.

Answering services are included in this category, but I generally do not recommend them, because the other alternatives are a lesser expense. If you know a good answering service that is affordable, though, that's great - use them.

Your Voicemail Greeting

People should come to know that they can rely on you to *quickly* return their calls and take care of their needs.

A sample message you could record is:

"You have reached Patricia Barnes. Please leave your name and number, and I'll return your call as soon as possible."

Use a voice message and not just an automated restatement of your phone number. Keep it short and to the point.

After you have recorded your outgoing message, listen to it carefully and objectively. Ask an honest friend to tell you how the message sounds. It should come across as lively and friendly, not monotone, dull or syrupy sweet. Keep recording it until it's suitable.

Speak slowly enough that people can understand what you are saying.

You might even consider doing some jumping jacks before recording your message to create a sense of excitement in your voice. That may sound silly but try it. You don't want your message to sound boring and doing jumping jacks will put energy in your voice! Also, smile as you record your message. It makes a difference!

Just be sure to keep the message professional. The message shouldn't be too cutesy, or it could confuse someone who's calling for the first time, looking for a possible employee.

Returning Messages

Always return a call, even if your work schedule is full and you're unable to accept the proposed assignment. I've had companies call six months in advance to schedule temporary work.

> **RETURN CALLS AS PROMPTLY AS POSSIBLE. DOING THIS MAY SOLVE ONE OF YOUR CLIENT'S PROBLEMS QUICKLY. AND YOU WANT TO BE THE ONE SOLVING THEIR PROBLEMS!**

Even if a company is calling you to work the following week and your schedule is already full, *return the call - quickly*. Doing so tells them that they can depend on you to return a call quickly and also provides you an opportunity to maintain contact with a company.

Whatever method you chose for hearing from your clients, I recommend keeping plenty of *current* printed materials with you at all times, in case one of those messages leads to a request for a business card or flyer. Having résumés or cards, with items crossed out and written in, does not project a professional image. Being caught without them could cost you a job!

Chapter 13 – Action Steps

1. Finalize your method of communicating, including establishing how you will keep track of this expense for a tax deduction.

14
ACCEPTING AN ASSIGNMENT

When you receive a call for an assignment, be sure to ask for and take notes on all pertinent information including:
- Verify the correct address.
- Special directions to the location.
- Parking instructions.
- Office hours.
- Who to ask for upon your arrival?
- Specifics about your job responsibilities.
- Any dress code or Covid routines.
- If this is a new client, add this information to your client list.

Before ending the call, make certain your contact knows your hourly rate. If they don't ask, tell them.

Send a follow-up email confirming all details.

When accepting a temporary position, refer to any personal business time you've already planned to take off as "prior commitments." Always inform the employer about any similar schedule variations - *before* you accept the assignment. Do not surprise them with a doctor's appointment at what might be a critical time for them. After following this rule, I only once had a problem getting time off for a prior commitment when the contact who scheduled me didn't tell her supervisor about it.

You'll occasionally receive a call from a company

requesting only one or two days of work. Tell them you prefer to work an entire week because short assignments make it difficult to find jobs to fill up the rest of the week.

Though I usually won't accept assignments shorter than a full week, doing so may work for you. I once accepted a two-day assignment when one of my regular clients called. Luckily, by the time I finished those days, another call came in for the remainder of the week.

Whether or not you accept a partial-week assignment is entirely up to you. Maybe you want to give yourself the three days off! But as previously stated, set a "minimum assignment length" for yourself.

Sometimes you will have requests for assignments from two to six months in advance. Mark these assignments on your calendar and call each organization a week or two *before* the actual assignment. Doing so confirms the assignment, but primarily lets the company know you haven't forgotten it.

Be sure to call your contact to confirm the assignment especially if another company wants to schedule you for the same week, informing them of the other company's request. This will let the organization know you're turning down work for their time slot.

Finally, a company might ask you to stop by for an hour or two the week before an assignment to preview the office layout, procedures, etc. Add these hours to the first statement you submit to the company, but not without first informing them you'll be doing so.

Chapter 14 – Action Steps

1. Establish an assignment acceptance routine.

15
PARKING

I've never requested paid parking because I've rarely incurred a parking fee. Here's how my parking fees have generally been covered:

Ask your contact, "Where should I park?" to which they may respond with one of the following:
- "Park in _____ garage, and we'll validate your parking ticket."
- "Park in _____ garage, and we'll give you the parking card of the person you're replacing."
- "Park in _____ garage, and we'll order you a temporary parking ticket."

If your contact offers a convenient place to park, but has not also provided any of the above options, you may want to ask if any of these options are available. Usually, downtown areas are where you'll have to be concerned about parking. Often, however, a company's building lease will require that employees, including temporary and/or contract employees, park in specified areas.

If you want to be reimbursed for any parking fee you incur, simply add on an extra 25 or 50 cents per hour to your rate to make up for the cost. Of course, in some industries, it's standard practice to charge an hourly fee plus expenses.

Some companies do not pay parking expenses for their regular employees, so expecting them to pay for yours as a

Freelance Temporary is not reasonable. If you pay for parking, keep records of how much each week, so you can deduct that amount from your taxes at the end of the year. You won't need a parking receipt each day for tax purposes, but it wouldn't hurt to have them. Just make a note in your calendar detailing your weekly parking fee.

Chapter 15 – Action Steps

1. Is there a phone app in your area which could direct you to cheap parking? Keep in mind – safety is the first priority.

2. Download an expense app or establish your method of keeping track of expenses. Taxbot is an option.

16
INSURANCE

Insurance costs are high but make having it a financial priority. One consolation to paying your own premiums is that insurance is a deductible expense for a self-employed person. Consider insurance a necessary expense.

Options for Heath Insurance

The following are a few sources for health insurance:
- Your spouse's policy – it might allow you to be added for a fee.
- Carry-over coverage – if you're planning on quitting a permanent position, check into this option before you do so. While it requires that you pay the premiums and is only available for a certain period of time, it will still probably be at a better rate than you could get on your own. Closely check any restrictions to this type of insurance.
- The Yellow Pages or the internet – look for an insurance agent who writes group policies for individual contractors. You may have a waiting period of about six months or more to show some type of consistency working as a Freelance Temp.
- Your personal auto or homeowner's insurance agent – since they already carry your other policies, they should be willing to provide you with a referral as a courtesy or write

one themselves. However, health insurance policies are difficult to handle, and agents receive no commission for writing them, so they usually only provide policies as an accommodation to an existing account.
- Association memberships – this may well be one of your best options. Certain associations, such as NASE.org says they "work with outside health insurance brokerages to provide access to health plans, but they vary by state."

Workers' Compensation

Workers' Compensation Insurance covers employees for injuries incurred "on the job." Google "workers compensation insurance" for currently available options. Some states do not require you to carry Workers' Compensation if you are self-employed and have no workers other than yourself. Your auto insurance company may be able to write this up for you but you will not need it if you have no other employees.

Chapter 16 – Action Steps

1. Contact your insurance company for a quote on Workers' Compensation coverage rates.
2. Google "workers compensation insurance." Check all potential sources for insurance.
3. Which of the above options will work best for you?

17
ADVERTISING

If you use each of the methods for finding work as described in this book, expenditures for advertising will be minimal, if anything at all.

The only advertising I recommend doing is on Craigslist, but before we discuss that, let's get the other options out of the way.

> **IF YOU WILL USE THE TECHNIQUES I HAVE GIVEN IN THIS BOOK, YOU SHOULD NOT HAVE TO PAY MUCH FOR ADVERTISING!**

If you truly wish to advertise, look for the magazine or newspaper that will reach the type of company you want to work for, as well as the type of company that needs your services.

I have advertised only twice, to find a part-time evening position. Most of my work had been for attorneys, so I advertised in the local "Legal Advocate," a publication for attorneys. Most of the responses I received were people who thought *I* wanted to hire extra help, so the ads did not generate any positive responses.

It probably would not be worthwhile to purchase an ad in your local Yellow Pages. Not only do you possibly have to have a "business" phone, but also the ads are quite expensive. In my opinion, this type of ad is just an unnecessary expense. But keep all your information current on your Yelp listing, your website, LinkedIn and other listings that have your information.

Craigslist

www.craigslist.org is a website where anyone can advertise for free using a very easy format. However, you must be careful when listing your experience in your ad. I once posted an ad listing each legal area in which I had experience (from working in law offices). My ad was flagged (deleted) because someone thought I was simply listing keywords, a practice which is not allowed on Craigslist.

Chapter 17 – Action Steps

1. Post your work experience on www.indeed.com and other internet resources listed in Chapter 9. Always keep a current list of these posts and always keep the information up-to-date.

18
DEALING WITH LARGE COMPANIES

There are three main problems you might encounter when dealing with a large company:
- They insist on working through an agency.
- They're concerned about hiring someone without workers' compensation.
- Their systems of processing your statements and issuing your checks involve a greater amount of red tape.

Working as An Agency

If you have a company name, you can represent yourself as a company or "temporary staffing agency," which can get you past the "having to work through an agency" problem. Check your state's requirements in regard to what is required for establishing a "temporary agency or staffing agency."

As mentioned before, one reason a company might want to work exclusively through an agency is to avoid tax problems. If a person works for a company directly, the company is responsible for taking taxes out of that person's earnings. Writing a check out to a company name usually allows them to avoid the problem. This is a strong reason for having a company name.

If a company makes a check out to your personal name, and you earn more than a certain amount (established by law, currently $600) in that year, they are required to send you a 1099 form at the end of the year. Always have a W-9 available.

Some large companies have a culture of "tradition" and, accordingly, will insist on going through an agency because that's what they've always done. They have never come across your Freelance Temporary alternative, so your job may also be one of educating companies to this innovative choice. You ARE an agency, so this additional task should be no problem. Ask why they insist on going through an agency. Their answer will show you how to reassure them. Refer to Chapter 10 for suggestions on answering objections such as these.

Lack of Workers' Compensation Coverage

Another reason a company would prefer to work through an agency is that their temps are covered by Workers' Compensation, or Workers' Comp. Generally speaking, if you're injured while working on their premises, they could be liable. Workers' Comp covers their liability in such an accident. To get around this obstacle, offer to pay the premium for yourself, but ask the company to add you to their list of employees they submit to their insurance company for coverage. This is assuming your assignment will be long enough to make this worthwhile.

As far as obtaining Workers' Comp coverage for yourself, see Chapter 16. If you purchase your own policy, list your coverage number on your promotional flyer to show that you're covered.

Over the course of five years, I only had two companies ever mention Workers' Comp to me, one of which added me to their coverage list without even charging me for it. If a company wouldn't hire me because of my lack of coverage, I'd simply move on to the next company on my list.

Red Tape

Large companies usually have computer payroll systems, resulting in substantial amounts of red tape. This red tape often affects the ease and regularity of your receiving a check. Be clear about routine and requirements in this regard.

19
GETTING PAID ON TIME

We want to be sure we receive each of our checks on time. To facilitate that timeliness, we can provide certain information and use other tips that might be helpful to the employer when cutting your checks.

Information to Include on Your Invoice

- Invoice Number – Most companies like to be able to refer back to an invoice number, in case there's an issue with a bill. Also, if you ever have a question about your statement or check, having a reference invoice number will be most helpful when making your inquiry.
- Date – The date you submit your invoice.
- Name and address of company – Your company, that is.
- Brief description of services rendered – For example, I would list "Freelance Legal Assistant" services.
- Dates worked, number of hours worked each day, total number of hours worked – Show each specific number.
- Hourly rate – Put this amount next to the total number of hours worked.
- Total due – Your hourly rate multiplied by the total number of hours you worked.
- Space for approval signature – Your statement may have to be approved, probably by the person for whom you have

been working. Signatures provide verification that you worked those hours. Often a signature isn't necessary but having space for it can be helpful.

- Space for special instructions – You may wish to add instructions as to how you'd like to receive your check. For example, "Please deliver to ___'s desk." or "Please call me at Ext. ___ when check is ready." Providing these instructions on your invoice usually prevents them from automatically mailing your check.

Invoicing this way is so simple you won't even need invoice software.

Should You Use a Timesheet?

Agencies usually use a timecard system showing when you arrived for work, went out for lunch, returned from lunch, and left work, probably online. I typically do not use any type of timesheet or timecard, but rather summarize my hours worked each day. During my years as a Freelance Temporary, only three out of the approximate 40 companies I've worked for have had me complete a timesheet. A company may require this if they are going to bill a client for your time/services, e.g., an engineering firm or law firm.

However, your supervisor may greatly appreciate your itemizing the amount of time you spend on each project. For example, if you're working in a law office, you may be required to designate the time you spent on different clients. This type of record makes it convenient for the company you're working for to back-charge clients for your hours.

Obviously, if the company requires it of all their employees, more than likely you will be required to do so as well.

How Often Should You Invoice?

I bill *each* Friday (or the last day of the week for which I work for a company), even if I'm on a two to six-week assignment. The only exception to this rule is if I'm on a long-term assignment, in which case I'll adapt to the company payroll system, which is generally every two weeks.

When to Submit Your Invoice

When working for a company for the first time, listen closely for clues about their payroll system. If they cut checks by hand, there is usually no problem getting a check at any time. If they have a computer system that generates the checks, it usually takes longer to get paid.

Unless you have already discussed invoice submission, at about midway through the first week of your assignment, ask either the person you're working for, or the person who initially called you, and say:

> "I usually bill every Friday. When should I turn in my statement/invoice, so that I can have my check by the time I leave Friday?"

This is your decision. You may have no problem waiting several weeks for a company's system to get you paid.

One company instructed me to submit my statement on Wednesday, filling in estimated time for Thursday and Friday. Usually, submitting Friday morning allows sufficient time. If the company agrees to that time, be diligent about preparing your invoice the first thing on Friday (or whenever they have instructed you to do so).

Remember - when billing as a temporary staffing service, you may have to be paid just as they'd pay any other agency, possibly net 30 days/at the end of the month. Luckily, I never had to wait that long.

A company will usually work with you on your invoicing system, but if for some reason they can't or won't, you must accept their pay system. Just be sure your statements and work are documented, and that you've kept signed copies of all your invoices.

If you can't wait 30 days for a check, be sure to address this when accepting an assignment.

Ensure Timely Processing

On Friday, at about 2 p.m., find out who will be delivering your check. Then ask that person if they've received your statement yet. If they have, you'll know things are going according to schedule. If they haven't, the paperwork has probably been stalled, and you need to ask about it. Investigating in the early afternoon is better than waiting till 4:55 p.m. to find out someone has held up the process.

If for some reason you're not able to pick up your check before leaving for the weekend, make certain you have a copy of your approved statement with an authorized signature. "Authorized signature" indicates a signature executed by a person who can verify and approve that you worked those hours, as opposed to an employee you sat next to (unless that's all you can get). I personally have never had someone refuse to pay me, nor have I ever received a bad check.

Chapter 19 – Action Steps

1. Set up your invoice form. It can simply be something you type out on your letterhead as a Word document.
2. Make a decision on how you will keep track of your hours.

20
HANDLING BAD CHECKS AND NO PAYS

Please don't become overly concerned about these issues. I've *never* received a bad check, or had anyone refuse to pay me. But it's an issue that may come up, so you should be prepared to deal with it.

When you begin your first assignment with a company, you have the option to have your supervisor sign a contract with you. You can purchase a printed form contract from an office supply store or consult an attorney.

If you do not use a contract, be sure someone in authority signs and approves your invoice before submitting it for payment. This step is especially important if you are not able to pick up your check before leaving on a Friday afternoon.

I've never personally used a contract and have been fortunate enough not to have needed one. However, some companies may have a contract they'd like you to sign, especially since the IRS has become more stringent about differentiating between an employee and a person working as a contractor.

Hopefully, each of your assignments have been confirmed, at least by email.

Read any contract a company presents to you regarding your services for them.

If, after you have completed both a contract and an invoice, someone refuses to pay you, send them a letter or email with a copy of the invoice, demanding payment. Send the letter via certified mail, return receipt requested. Or fax the letter and statement, as a confirmation page from the fax is also considered proof of delivery. An email is also considered a valid agreement. If they still do not pay you, your next recourse will be a visit to Small Claims Court.

The maximum amount you can sue for in Small Claims Court may vary, depending on state and local laws, but $5,000.00 is typical. You will need to check this with your local court for the exact amount. Fortunately, this quantity should more than cover your invoice, which should encompass only one to two weeks of work. If they are not paying you, don't be manipulated into working for them longer than that.

When filing your claim, be sure to sue for the amount due, plus your court costs, plus the additional costs you've lost in missing time from work to file the claim. For example, see the following calculations:

Amount due you (40 hours x $30/hour)	$ 1,200.00
Court Costs (filing fee)	120.00
Lost wages to file claim (plan on about half a day, or 4 hours x $30/hour)	120.00
TOTAL AMOUNT OF CLAIM	$ 1,440.00

Before filing your claim, search the records at the Secretary of State's office to be sure you're filing the claim against the *incorporated* company name - the actual name under which the company is incorporated - which is not necessarily the name under which the company does business. (An incorporated company can also work under a d/b/a.)

Google "secretary of state [your state]" and find the database search feature. There may be a fee for using this option.

You can also file a complaint with the local Better Business Bureau - www.bbb.org

You can do all of this yourself. If your bill is quite large, however, it would probably be worthwhile to hire an attorney to pursue payment for you. Select an attorney who will work on a contingency fee basis, that is, one who only collects a certain percentage of what is ultimately collected. If you cannot find a lawyer who will take the suit on a contingency fee basis, you will have to settle for one who will ask for attorney fees as part of the lawsuit, so those fees will be reimbursed if your suit is successful.

If you get no results with the above suggestions, the only consolation would be that you can list the loss of funds as "bad debt" on your income tax return, using Schedule C. Attorney expenses are also deductible as a business expense.

Rather than putting yourself through such anguish, do not wait until a company owes you so much money!

Do not work for a company longer than a week or two if they are not paying you! If you find you are consistently having trouble collecting your fees, evaluate how you are handling your invoicing.

In some cases, it may be appropriate to require a "retainer fee" or "fee deposit" before you accept or begin a job. The amount would be up to you - possibly your materials cost, if you have any - or 25% of your estimated fee. A fee such as this would primarily be applicable for someone such as a window dresser, graphic designer, etc., or a person who produces a tangible item.

Send invoices often enough, and insist on payment often enough, so that in the event there *is* a bad check, it will not be for a large amount.

Chapter 20 – Action Steps

1. Keep current with your invoicing and payments.
2. Stop working for someone if they are not paying you!

21
MULTIPLE STREAMS OF INCOME

What some industries call "up-selling" or "cross-marketing" can generate "multiple streams of income." Having multiple streams of income suggests great wisdom and excellent business strategy.

Do you have some other income stream that you could possibly be promoting at your temporary jobs? For example, do you work part time repairing computers, or making beaded jewelry? Either of these hobbies could lead to substantial supplemental income.

Now I will quickly add - you must use *wisdom* and *common sense* when cross-marketing!

After you've gotten to know the company and some of the people who work there, you'll be able to tell the right time to mention your other income streams. Actually, it will probably come up naturally in the "getting to know you" conversation, as you work with other employees.

People are usually fascinated and interested in my freelance work, how I got started, etc. Any other business will just naturally come up. And, AT THE RIGHT TIME, ask about promoting your other opportunity. Using the examples above, find out who you should talk to about meeting computer repair needs or setting up a jewelry display during lunch one day.

22
FIVE SIMPLE KEYS TO GENERATE REPEAT BUSINESS

Although you'll constantly be generating *new* business, *repeat* business is very important. Since, as a Freelance Temporary, you are finding your own work, someone calling you back to work for them will help keep your work schedule full, without much effort on your part. Repeat business should constitute a major part of your work. Gaining repeat business is actually a simple process:
- CARE.
- Do good work and do it willingly.
- Be flexible and fit in with company routines and procedures.
- Go "the extra mile."
- ASK for repeat business!

Sounds quite simple doesn't it? Well, it is. When I first started as a Freelance Temporary, I thought about all of the occasions I'd had as a supervisor, using temporary help, and how most of them had been a bad experience. I considered the temporary help's poor work habits and bad attitudes made it such a displeasure to work with them. At that point, I determined that I would change the reputation of the office "temp."

I decided I wouldn't do all of the things temps had done while working for me: getting to work anywhere from 30 minutes to two hours late, taking two or three hours for lunch, griping and complaining about the work that was given to them, etc. Of course, not all temps are like that. Ask employers about the experiences they've had with conventional temporary help — it'll be an education to hear them. When I asked, their stories meshed with my experiences and I decided that I would not be like those irresponsible and disagreeable temps I was familiar with.

1. Care.

Care whether or not you do a good job. It's pleasant to see how totally *delighted* a company is just to have a temp who will get to work on time, accomplish her work willingly and return within the given lunchtime. Simply be a good worker!

If you're going to take some time off during the week a company has asked you to work — whether it's for a full personal day or only an hour for a dental appointment — inform them of that time off *before* you accept the job assignment. For example, if you'll need a Tuesday off and someone calls you to work that week say, "Yes, I can work that week, but I already have a commitment for Tuesday. If you'd like me to work the other four days, I'm free then." Do not surprise them and throw them off schedule more than they already are. Allow them to be able to PLAN for these events. Let them know, as far in advance as possible, that you must be off a certain time.

When asked a question, never say, "I'm just a temp." It's easy to fall back on this response. Sure, you may have only been working at the company for two hours or two days, but to use the cop-out of "I'm just a temp" and leave it at that is an expression of the "I don't care" attitude. It's saying, "I don't know the answer and I don't care whether I know or find out." If you don't know the answer, *ask someone*. It may be a question you'll be asked again later anyway.

2. Do Good Work and Do It Willingly.

The question has often come up, "Does a temp have the 'right' to refuse to do certain work?" If you are caught up with your work and something needs to be done, do it. At the same time, there are people in some companies who will try to take advantage of temps and give them their unwanted tasks. I will help out if I'm not busy, but I won't be taken advantage of, nor will I do someone else's work just because they don't want to do it.

If you are asked to do work you weren't hired to do and that is not at all within your job scope, discuss it with the person you're working for. For example, if you were hired as a receptionist, but were then expected to do filing that hindered your attention to the phones, do not feel out of line to discuss this with your supervisor. By making your own work arrangements, you will be able to avoid most of these situations if you get a clear idea of your responsibilities when accepting a freelance assignment.

Another question that often arises is — "If I'm not busy, is it OK to read during an assignment?" At first, I was concerned about this. If I had completed all of my work, and let my supervisor know I was caught up, perhaps even checked with the employee working next to me to see if she needed help, and there was no work for me to do - I went ahead and asked if I could read, type a personal letter. There was never any problem with this, so I always carry a book or my phone with me. (Be extremely conscious of any of your personal equipment. Never leave it just sitting around.) If I have verified all these points, I take out my book and read. Some temp jobs are not busy jobs. Companies usually realize you don't have much to do and are more comfortable with your keeping yourself occupied, instead of sitting there looking bored.

3. Be Flexible and Fit in with *Their* Routines and Procedures.

Realize the position your employer is in. Your supervisor is off routine because her regular assistant — that person who always knew where the files were, just how the supervisor liked things done, and all office procedures and routines - is out. Make it as easy for them as possible. Adapt to the company's procedures and routines.

Know who your supervisor is in the company and the chain of command. As a Freelance Temp, you have the option of stating your hours, but doing this might limit some of your assignments. The choice is up to you.

Acclimate yourself to whatever letter or memo style they use. Don't go into a company and try to change their procedures, routines and filing systems. This is not to say you cannot offer suggestions or share new ideas. Just keep in mind that if they'd hired you to organize the office or set procedures, you would have known that in advance.

Know your priorities and don't be afraid to ask questions. It takes less time to ask and/or answer a "dumb" question than to correct a "dumb" mistake.

It's also a good idea to adjust your attire to whatever dress code they may have. Some companies, especially law firms, may still prefer a conservative look. If that's the case, be conservative. Dressy casual may initially be appropriate until you are familiar with any dress code a company may have. Ask about a dress code when accepting an assignment.

4. Go the Extra Mile

If you have followed the points listed above, you've already accomplished this goal to some extent. You may not have been very busy, so you offered to help the employee next to you. There are many other things you can do to "go the extra mile." Don't wait to be told to do everything. After you've picked up on the routine, keep your work current. Maintain a stock of supplies for you and your supervisor. Clean your area or the equipment you're working with, being especially careful with delicate equipment that requires special training to operate.

When you leave an assignment, be sure the stationery, envelopes and other supplies at your desk are well stocked. Sharpen all the pencils. Leave the desk neat and clean. Check to see if you need to water any plants in the office. Doing a little more than is required of you will go a long way in making a favorable and memorable impression and it will greatly increase your chances of getting repeat business.

5. *Ask* **for Repeat Business!**

You will generally find that if you follow the suggestions stated above, the company will have already told you they'll be calling you again. Tell them you would love to work for them again. Leave a card with each person at the company who might have occasion to need your services later. Even if you're working at a company for the fourth time, employees change and cards get lost, so leave a new card with whomever you might deem appropriate.

Obtain the email address of everyone you have had contact with before your final day on assignment.

Check with your contact before you leave to see if someone has a vacation coming up - she might schedule you as her replacement on the spot.

Maintain contact with the company. If later on, you're working in that part of town, call someone you worked with and have lunch together. Be sure to clarify if you mean a "Dutch treat." Especially if you are looking for work, call the places where you've previously worked. Ask for referrals to other companies in their building, area, or industry.

Chapter 22 – Action Steps

1. Gather email addresses and extension numbers of everyone you were in contact with, especially those who hire the

temporary help. Get them on your email system, with their permission.
2. Leave a business card with each person you are in contact with.
3. *Ask* for repeat business!

23
WHAT IF A COMPANY WANTS TO CANCEL YOUR ASSIGNMENT WITHOUT NOTICE?

This has happened to me three times, twice on six-week assignments and once near the end of a four-month assignment. The first time it happened, the company had asked me to work for them for six weeks. I accepted the assignment and began the job. Another client called for me to work for them during that time, but I turned them down since my current assignment was to last six weeks. One Friday afternoon, about three weeks into the assignment, my supervisor said they didn't have the project ready for me and wouldn't be needing my services any longer.

When this happened, I didn't just drop the issue then and there. Rather, I reminded my supervisor that I had refused other work because of my commitment to them. Then, I offered to call the other company that had asked me to work for them to see if they still needed help, but they had already found someone else. I reported this to my supervisor.

Neither of us had signed a contract. They were not legally bound to keep me on. But I appealed to their ethical and moral nature to keep their commitment to me, as I had to them. They kept me on, finding a different project for me to work on.

Hopefully, you have confirmed this assignment via email. Refer them to that email.

Other than a confirming email, I personally do not use

contracts unless a company requests one. If I am on a long-term assignment and get a call for another assignment, I check with my current supervisor before turning down the new request. I inform them that I have another call for my services and would like to be sure they will continue to need my services before turning the other assignment down. Even though I have confirmed all agreements via email, this lets them know I am turning work down.

24
FINDING WORK TO FILL A FREE WEEK

Until you have established a reliable client list with repeat business coming in, you'll be calling companies to find your own work.

The months from December until March consistently mark my "slow time." Other Freelance Temps have found the summer to be their slow time. Slow periods will vary with your client list and industry. Some companies are very busy at year-end, while others gear down at that time, awaiting the new year.

When a week without scheduled work is approaching, follow these seven steps (unless you're going to give yourself a vacation!):

1. Call your main contact at your "specialty" company, the business selling the product in which you specialize. Ask if they have heard of anyone who might need help. Let them know you're looking for work that week so if they hear from someone, they can specifically refer them to you.
2. Call your most recent contacts. Review the copies of the emails/letters you've sent out. Call the people who have most recently called you to see if they still need help. Call those who called you a month or so earlier.
3. Check the classified ads in your local newspaper. Call the ones you think might need temporary help.
4. Check all internet resources and search your local Craigslist

for job postings. Reply to posts, asking if they need temporary help until they hire someone permanent.
5. Call any other temps you know to see if they can give you a lead on jobs they weren't able to fill.
6. Call your friends to see if their companies need any temporary help.
7. If, by this time, you do not have work, start calling everyone on your client list. You also can contact them by email or messaging. However, by calling you will immediately know their response. They will be reminded of you. With email they may not even open it. You won't know if you've made contact.

> "This is Patricia Barnes. I spoke with you recently about working temporary as a legal assistant (or, I have worked temp for you before). I'm free this week and just checking to see if you need help."

You can also send out emails. I prefer calls because then I'll know if someone is no longer at the company.

Following these steps will usually turn up someone who needs help. And even if it doesn't, you've touched base with a number of individuals, so they'll more than likely think of you first when they *do* need help.

I have only called through my entire client list a couple of times without finding an assignment by the next day.

Also, I typically only have about three weeks per year when I don't have an assignment. One year I had four Monday mornings in which I got to sleep in before making calls to generate work.

You'll notice that most of the points above contain the word call, call, and call. The only instances when I have had free time (that I didn't want) was when I did NOT make those calls! As long as you keep calling, you should be able to find someone who needs you.

When I first started working temporary positions, I did not

have any work after my initial four-month assignment. I sat around depressed for about a week. Then, I started making phone calls. I found a company that needed help — and they had needed help the previous week, too! If I had been making my calls, I would have been working!

Don't forget to plan your financial budget to cover times when you may not be able to find work for a week, but also learn to *enjoy* the time off you have. Don't panic. Do something productive. Keep making your calls, but take pleasure in that time off.

As you are making your calls, make an effort to keep your client list current. Companies move. Employees change. Enter all new information into Outlook or whatever system you use for your contacts, so you'll always have the correct phone number and person to ask for when you call.

In April of each year, I have called all my clients to see if they have any summer vacations scheduled for which they would like to schedule temporary help. The question typically generated responses like, "____ wants to take the first two weeks of August, but she has to wait to see if her husband can take off." Then, I offer to pencil her in for those two weeks. If I get another assignment opportunity for that time, I call them back, either to obtain a firm commitment or to cancel the job. Doing so allows me to take care of my steady clients first, as well as fill up my schedule.

Chapter 24 – Action Steps

1. Call! Call! Call! Make those calls. Someone needs your help today.
2. As you call, update your client list.

25
RECORDS TO KEEP

Copies of Your Invoices

You will present a statement, or invoice, for services rendered to each of your clients. Keep a copy of each one of these. Also keep a copy of any timesheet you have filled out. Scan and keep a copy of each signed invoice.

Check Stubs

When my check is delivered to me, I immediately detach the check from the stub and staple the stub to my copy of its corresponding invoice. I also make a note of the check number, bank name, and account number, if the information isn't already printed on the stub. Doing this is what Uncle Sam calls keeping "proof of income." If there is no stub attached to my check, I write on my copy of the invoice "Paid by Check No. ___" and note the name of the bank and the account number.

Add these statements up at the end of the year for your total income.

Be sure to separate out the invoices of the companies that send you a 1099-Misc. form, so that you do not add your income twice. When applying for a loan, the loan company will ask to see the 1099-Misc. forms as proof of income for that year.

Copy of All Correspondence

Keep copies of all letters you have written to people who've contacted you for work, especially if you were NOT able to provide them temporary services when they needed it. Include letters you have initiated to find work.

Tax Receipts

I'll explain which receipts you need to keep in the following chapter.

Client List

Always maintain a client list with current addresses and phone numbers. I've mentioned it numerous times, but it bears repeating. This list should include:

- All companies to which you send a business card
- Any prospective client from whom you have received a positive response when introduced to your company
- Any company for which you have worked
- Any company you found in the newspaper that needed your service
- Any company to which your friends referred you

Keep this list updated with your contacts at each company. All information can be of great assistance under many circumstances. For example, when returning for an assignment at a company you haven't worked for in two or three years — at this juncture, that information could help you shine even before you begin your excellent work.

Chapter 25 – Action Steps

1. Establish a record/receipt file system if you haven't done so already.

26
UNCLE SAM WANTS HIS SHARE

Quarterly Estimated Taxes

As a self-employed person, you'll pay taxes quarterly to the IRS, using Form No. 1040ES. The top portion of this document shows you how, in a complicated manner, to figure what your quarterly estimated payments will be. However, there is a much simpler way to calculate this sum.

The main principle involved: You have to pay, in *estimated* taxes, *this* year, at least as much in taxes as you paid *last* year.

In other words, if you paid $2,000 in taxes last year, you'll have to pay at least that much as your *estimated* taxes. Divide that number by four to get the quarterly amount. Take that new number and divide it by the number of weeks in that quarter to get the amount you will need to SAVE out of your weekly checks in order to cover your taxes in full. Following our example above, you would simply divide the $2,000 by four, then divide that amount by 13 (or the number of weeks you plan to work) to give you the amount you need to SAVE from your check EACH WEEK. If you use the instructions on Form 1040ES, you may end up paying more than necessary. The form shows you when the quarterly payment is due.

However, when your temporary business is really taking off, you'll want to pay the estimated taxes on a higher income bracket, so you won't have an exorbitant tax bill next April.

SAVE MONEY to Pay Your Estimated Taxes!

The most important advice I can give you about taxes as a self-employed person is: SAVE the money to pay your estimated payments from the beginning! And pay them on time!

Heed the painful words of experience you are reading right now! I did not do this and what a mess.

You are probably used to having a company automatically take out your taxes, and because of that, it would be very easy to take your whole check and spend it, not thinking to save any for your quarterly estimated taxes. Doing this will cause a great strain on your budget when it comes time to make your estimated payment.

Some people think they'll just save their money until the end of the year, then pay their taxes from the interest they've earned on their savings. You can do this, but then you'll also have to pay a "failure to estimate" penalty & interest fee on the money Uncle Sam would have had if you'd paid your taxes on time. The penalty & interest will amount to more than you will have earned in interest in *any* savings account. And, if you are unable to pay quarterly, you will continue to have to pay a "failure to pay" penalty on your unpaid amount until the time that you do pay.

Take care of this from the start and save yourself a lot of money, stress and frustration.

Tax Identification Number

Some companies may ask you for your "tax identification number," or a tax ID. This number is primarily required of a person who has other people working for her, so it's not a necessity, since you're the only person your "agency" sends out. Of course, if you give them a W-9, they will have your social security number.

There is no charge to apply for a tax ID, so feel free to do so if you'd like. Search for Form SS-4 online or pick up a copy at your local IRS office.

Note that your social security number serves as your tax ID because you're the only person in your agency. Consult your accounting professional to see if there is any reason they would recommend your using a tax ID number, other than your social security number.

Tax Deductions

As a self-employed person, deduct all of your business expenses on Schedule C with Form 1040 whether or not you itemize or take the standard deduction.

However, you decide to take your deduction, you should still deduct your business expenses.

The following is a list of business expenses you can deduct:
- Business stationery, business cards, postcards, brochures.
- Postage – Count the copies of your letters at the end of the year and multiply that number by the cost of postage.
- Parking, car repair expenses, gas, depreciation, etc. (but only if you do not use the mileage deduction) – this deduction is only available to individuals who must drive in order to offer overtime work to their clients; (i.e., people who would not be able to get from one job to the next in the same day to work overtime by riding the bus).
- Mileage – You can either deduct the actual car expenses mentioned in the previous bulleted item or take a standard mileage deduction. I have found it to be less cumbersome and of a greater savings to take the standard mileage deduction. Bear in mind that you can only use the standard mileage deduction if your vehicle has not been fully depreciated.
- Insurance – medical, disability.
- Advertising.
- A portion of phone expense – this includes an answering

service if you use one. Your entire phone expense is deductible if you have a business line.
- Memberships to professional organizations and subscriptions to industry journals.
- A portion of your home for office space. The IRS is very strict about this. The room must be used *strictly* as an office.
- Office supplies.
- Tax preparation fees, or TurboTax-type software cost.
- Cell phone usage – For your cell phone expense, multiply your total cell phone bill by the percentage of time it was used for your business. This is the amount of your cell phone deduction. Confirm this with your tax accountant.
- Any bad debts and/or attorney fees.
- The cost of this book – if you're working as a Freelance Temp or you, in fact, start your own business.

KEEP TRACK OF YOUR EXPENSES using this guideline: If an expense is under $25, you do not have to show a receipt for verification, but you must show some sort of consistent record for such expenditures. For example, at the end of each week on your calendar, note your parking fees for that week. However, it would be simple to have a file and throw your receipts in it as you get them.

Using MapQuest, Yahoo maps or Google maps or your GPS provides you with exact mileage. Go to www.mapquest.com or www.googlemaps.com; click "Get Directions" and enter your beginning location and the location of your assignment.

If your wages (per company) were over $600 for that year, and they make your check out to your personal name instead of your company name, companies are required to send you a 1099 form. It is the company's responsibility to send this to you, but if they do not, use your invoice and pay stub as proof of income.

Most of these expenses will be minimal. Do not raise a red flag to the IRS by listing excessive expenses. The rule is "ordinary and necessary."

Have a Tax Specialist Prepare Your Tax Return

There may be other deductions you can use, depending on your situation, so check these with your tax specialist.

Consider having a professional prepare your taxes if you're involved with complicated tax issues. It is difficult enough for a CPA to keep current on all the changing tax laws, let alone a layperson. Professionals are better trained to know what you can and cannot deduct. Professional tax preparers are expensive, but sometimes they can save you money and are thus most worthwhile.

Turbo Tax

Software like TurboTax is quite detailed in its instructions and deductions; I've used it to file my taxes.

Chapter 26 – Action Steps

1. Obtain Form 1040-ES for your estimated taxes.
2. Pay your estimated quarterly taxes!
3. Be diligent with noting expenses and saving receipts.

27
CONQUER YOUR FEARS

Well - that's it, as far as how to start your business! So, what are we left with? Having walked the path you are contemplating; I know the answer to this question. We are left with your fears. There are several you need to address and process.

What could some of these fears be?
- I have a family to support. I HAVE to have a regular paycheck.
- I'm not a salesperson, and I'm not comfortable "selling" myself.
- I don't have marketing skills.
- I can't imagine anyone ever calling or using me.

TAKING ACTION TAKES THE STING OUT OF FEAR

Here are some possible corresponding resolutions to those fears:
- Figure how many hours you would have to work temporarily to earn at least what you're making at your current job and set that amount as your minimum goal. Doing this will help you realize your goal by breaking it down into concrete parts and making it seem more

accessible.
- If you don't feel as though you have sales talent, try contacting people in the way you're most comfortable - over the phone is easiest, the least time consuming, and the most effective way. After all, what's the worst thing that could happen to you on a phone call? If you can't handle "cold calling," start an email campaign.
- If you are marketing your actual skills to the people who need those skills, this fear is well proven to be unrealistic.

All I'm saying to you is tell yourself the truth!
You have the skills.
You have your list of clients – the companies who need you.
So, *take action* based on the TRUTH!

Ask yourself: Would the results of your fears becoming reality, coupled with the benefits of working temporarily, still outweigh your current job frustrations? In other words, working for yourself may be worthwhile, even if your fears become reality.

Build a wide foundation of support. Do not look to only one person. Then, make a list of those people and meet or talk with them on a regular basis. This list could include members of your professional association, as well as your networking group. Your list should include anyone who has ever given you leads or ideas for your business.

Is there a Facebook group for your job/industry?

Ask for help and encouragement from your group, but don't look for support where you've sought it before and never gotten it. If you mention your project to someone who responds in a negative fashion, don't include that person on your list of supporters!

Save as much money as you can to serve as a buffer in case of an emergency.

Give your business a trial run — work temporary on your vacation time. Or try it out during what you know will be the busy season for your type of work (e.g., admin work - summer; accounting - tax time). Summer would be a good time for a teacher to try out temporary work in a new field.

If you quit or lose a job, you have the ideal opportunity to test the waters. *Remember:* Working temporary is a great way to find a permanent job!

You don't have to be out of work to complete the start-up steps discussed in Chapters 2 and 3.

Don't get bogged down in the non-productive stuff like buying letterhead. Make the calls!

The bottom line: You *will* be taking a risk by making this attempt at self-employment. But the rewards can be tremendous!

So ... what are your first steps?

This **Quick-Start Action Plan** has only FOUR steps:
1. Decide what service you're offering.
2. Have business cards made.
3. Determine who needs your services and start your client list.
4. Immediately start calling/contacting the companies that need your services!

Getting started is really that simple!

Hopefully, you've worked your way through the Action Steps at the end of each chapter and are well on your way to developing your business.

Working temporary can be exciting, stimulating, educational and very rewarding! You can gain exposure to several areas of employment and work with many people. Not everyone will work temporary in their career years. Instead of being stuck in one job, not knowing where it will take you, or even where you want it to take you, temporary work offers you variety and many other advantages to help you better determine your career direction.

THIS PROCESS WORKS! GIVE IT A TRY!
Then let me know how much you love it.

GOOD LUCK!

Chapter 27 – Action Steps

1. List the people who you believe will support you in your new business. Call them and let them know *how* they can actively support you.
2. Join my private Facebook group for support for those who have read this book:

www.bit.ly/FindTemporaryJobs

www.ingramcontent.com/pod-product-compliance
Lightning Source LLC
Chambersburg PA
CBHW070643050426
42451CB00008B/284